WINDOWS ON RUSSIA AND EASTERN EUROPE

WINDOWS ON RUSSIA AND EASTERN EUROPE

Graduates tell their stories of life, work and survival

edited by Phil Davis

Bramcote Press
Ilkeston, Derbyshire
2013

© Phil Davis and authors of signed contributions 2013

All rights reserved. No reproduction, copy or transmission of the whole or part of this publication may be made without written permission.

First published 2013 by
**Bramcote Press,
81 Rayneham Road,
ILKESTON,
Derbyshire
DE7 8RJ
United Kingdom**

Printed by Berforts Information Press Ltd, Stevenage

ISBN 978-1-900405-21-8

Contents

Foreword
    Richard Owen   vii
Preface
    Malcolm Jones   ix
Editor's Introduction
    Phil Davis   xi

I. Cold War capers

Inside the bell jar
    Jonathan Bastable   1
Games about frontiers
    Terry Sandell   19

II. Change, chaos and cowboy capitalism

The Wild East
    Daniel Vowles   27
Military games and capitalist capers
    Will Stamper   35
All the world's a stage
    Rachel Farmer   51
Crime, punishment and investigative psychology
    Marion Bates   63

III. Fissures and fireworks

Staying alive in the siege of Sarajevo
    Rod Thornton   71
Taking the bus
    Vanessa Pupavac   93
Monitoring the media
    Colin Davison   103

IV. Resistance to change persists

The Ghost of St Petersburg past
    Hannah Collins   113
A Cry from Solovki
    John Butler   119
Excess and contradiction in Russia
    Daniel Kearvell   133

V. Life-long addicts

The Road less travelled
    Keith Watkinson   149
High notes, low notes
    John Culley   159

Illustrations

Several contributors and others have kindly provided copyright photographs and images for the cover of this book and for the illustrations. In particular we thank Daniel Vowles, Will Stamper, Rachel Farmer, Marion Bates, Rod Thornton, Hannah Collins, John Butler, Daniel Kearvell, John Culley, and Malcolm Jones.

For the front cover design we are indebted to Jayne Amat.

Foreword

by Richard Owen

WHEN I arrived at Nottingham to study Russian in the mid 1960s, I could scarcely have imagined I would find myself some fifteen years later reporting from Moscow for *The Times*. But as this fascinating volume shows, studying a language leads inevitably to an involvement in – not to say a passion for – the culture and history of the country (or countries) where that language is spoken.

In my case I went to the London School of Economics after Nottingham to study Soviet politics, and was subsequently taken on by the BBC Overseas Service (then just across the road from the LSE at Bush House) to run its Russian broadcasts on current affairs. I eventually transferred to *The Times,* which in 1982 sent me to Moscow – just in time to record for readers, and perhaps for posterity (what the *Washington Post* once termed 'the first rough draft of history') the transitions in the Kremlin from Brezhnev to Andropov, Chernenko and Gorbachev.

The narratives in this book tell similar tales of professional and personal entanglement with Russia and Eastern Europe – not just during the Cold War and what turned out to be the dying days of the Soviet system, but also the period of 'gangster capitalism' which followed when Soviet power collapsed, up to the present rather uneasy post-Communist Russian mixture of market forces and semi-liberty coupled with resurgent nationalism and authoritarian rule. There are tales too of the fratricidal and ethnic violence which followed the breakdown of Communist control in Eastern Europe, notably in Bosnia and the former Yugoslavia.

What shines through however is not only the negative aspect of dealing with the KGB, the Russian Mafia, military paranoia or the darker side of nationalism, but also the enduring enchantment of Slav literature, music, spiritual values and warmth of character: one contributor, Daniel Kearvell, even married a Russian girl, which is deep immersion indeed – even if, as he notes, he is still to some extent an 'outsider'.

As I also found in Russia, and during my post-Moscow career in other foreign postings for *The Times,* immersion in a foreign country or region does not mean you become accepted by its inhabitants as 'one of them'; how could it? What it does do is to enrich one's life and career immeasurably through involvement in another world – in the case of Russia and Eastern Europe, a world of unmatched culture and history, hospitality and friendship, and intense intellectual and spiritual stimulation.

And the key to entering that world is language. My experience in forty years of journalism is that business leaders, politicians, cultural figures all deal with you quite differently if you speak their language. You may still be an 'outsider' – but you have an inside track which those without language skills can only guess at, and which (with luck) lasts a lifetime.

Richard Owen graduated in Modern Languages (Russian and German Joint Honours) from Nottingham University in 1969. He was awarded an MSc with distinction in Government and Politics from the London School of Economics in 1971, followed by a PhD on Russian Political History at the LSE based on research conducted at the Hoover Institution at Stanford University in California during a Harkness Fellowship in the US. He joined the BBC in 1973, working in the Overseas Service and subsequently in BBC Television current affairs before joining The Times in 1980 as a leader writer. He served as bureau chief in Moscow from 1982, in Brussels from 1985 and in Jerusalem from 1988, during the first Palestinian intifada and the First Gulf War. He returned to London in 1991 to become Foreign Editor of The Times *for five years before returning to the field, this time in Rome, to cover Italy, the Vatican and the Mediterranean and Balkans. His publications include Crisis in the Kremlin: Soviet Succession and Rise of Gorbachev, Letters from Moscow, The Times Guide to the Single European Market and The Times Guide to World Organisations. He retired in September 2010 after covering the papal trip to the UK by Pope Benedict XVI.*

Preface

WHEN collecting material for *Slavianskii mir, the story of Slavonic Studies at the University of Nottingham in the twentieth century* (published in 2009), I corresponded with a wide range of alumni about their memories of studying Russian there. Without being asked, some of them volunteered information about their experiences in Russia and Eastern Europe following graduation, some of it highly colourful and engaging. It soon became clear that there was a new book here that might be of interest not only to fellow Nottingham graduates but also to a much wider readership of students, teachers, lecturers, careers advisers, and even prospective employers, all those in fact with an interest in the possibility of living and working in the region after graduation.

Even today one hears sceptics questioning the value of learning a foreign language and studying foreign cultures, and of the chances of finding a career in which they may be used. The essays in this book show how such studies have opened doors and enhanced the lives of their authors in a wide range of experiences and adventures, and continue to do so to this day. We hope that one result of publishing this book may be to lay to rest some of the monolingual prejudices that often diminish and impoverish our life experiences and disadvantage us in our dealings with the Slavonic peoples.

At about the same time, Phil Davis had had a similar idea. We decided to work as a team, Dr Rachel Farmer and I (both Nottingham alumni, like Phil) initially soliciting essays through the good offices of the Alumni Office, with Phil ultimately taking over responsibility for editing and bringing the book to fruition. The final member of the core team was Dr James Muckle, at the time Honorary Professor in Education at Nottingham, but for many years responsible for training teachers of Russian in its Education Faculty, whose Bramcote Press had published *Slavianksii mir*, and who has published the present volume as well.

There are many people to whom we owe a debt of gratitude: firstly to the contributors, both for their essays and the patience with which they have dealt with our queries; secondly to Jayne Amat, who has been a model of forbearance, for the cover design; thirdly to Emeritus Professor Lesley Milne for copy-editing and, not least, to James Muckle who has guided us through the intricacies of publication and dealt with the business side of the process, in addition to showing a lively interest in the contents from start to finish. Finally, we were delighted when Dr Richard Owen, himself a graduate of the department, who worked as *Times* Correspondent in Moscow from 1982 to 1985, agreed so readily to write the Foreword.

Malcolm V. Jones
Nottingham 2013

Malcolm Jones graduated in Russian Studies at the University of Nottingham in 1962 (PhD 1966). Following a brief period lecturing at the new University of Sussex, he returned to Nottingham in 1967, eventually becoming Professor of Slavonic Studies and head of department in 1980. Before his retirement in 1997, he visited Russia and the former Yugoslavia many times and is the author of books and articles on Russian literature and intellectual history. At the University he served twice as Dean of the Arts Faculty and also as Pro-Vice-Chancellor. He was a member of various national and international committees with interests in Slavonic Studies and the wider humanities, and for ten years was General Editor of Cambridge Studies in Russian Literature. He is probably best known for his publications on Dostoevsky, and was President of the International Dostoevsky Society from 1995 to 1998.

Editor's Introduction

THE narratives in this book represent individuals' tales of how the Communist-controlled lands of the Soviet Union and Eastern Europe evolved from Stalinism to Gorbachev's *perestroika* to the robber baron days of the 1990s and finally to today's uneasy mix of free markets and semi-authoritarian rule. The stories are those of graduates of Slavonic studies, who chose to live and work in the former USSR and Communist Eastern Europe. Setting off on their chosen path in Slav lands, the authors were typically well-versed in terms of language and culture. But many underestimated the challenges – and dangers – they would encounter. Their stories, I hope you'll agree, make compelling reading.

The narratives punctuate the recent history of great and troubled lands. In telling their stories, the narrators and (sometimes) protagonists also lay bare the nature of the Slav peoples. They are possessed of weaknesses to be sure, but also unusual warmth, unique resilience and a peculiarly downbeat love of life.

Part I – Cold War capers

The first part of this book focuses on pre-perestroika Soviet Union and its obsession with low-level espionage. Whereas the Stalin era had been characterized by execution, exile and expulsion, the latter Soviet period seemed to be characterised by a pettier form of the spygame.

In the first narrative, **Jonathan Bastable**'s KGB case officers, for example, go to considerable lengths to 'catch him out'. In echoes of Orwell's *1984*, he is often treated kindly. But Bastable was never a spy, so why did the KGB take such a close interest in him?

Behind the sabre-rattling and the rhetoric, the Cold War was played out in endless rounds of tit-for-tat expulsions and spygames. Diplomat **Terry Sandell** becomes an unwitting participant and meets pre-presidential Putin, and prime ministers Wilson and Thatcher in the process.

Part II – Change, chaos and cowboy capitalism

The stage for the second part is those crucial few years of change in the 1990s, when the Berlin Wall suddenly fell and the Communist regime unexpectedly collapsed. The political changes led to freer contact between East and West while the economic changes paved the way for frenetic and frightening cowboy capitalism. The changes provided opportunities for some, but led to misery for others. **Daniel Vowles** finds himself caught up in the overnight transformation of the black markets of Communist into unfettered, uncontrolled capitalism. His description invites comparisons with the American Wild West of the mid-1800s.

Meanwhile, **Will Stamper**, in his roles as a military adviser and an executive at a banknote printing company, also testifies to the alarming reduction in personal security that accompanied sudden democracy.

Nevertheless, business – possibly for the first time in Soviet and Russian history – was possible on terms Western individuals and companies could recognise. **Rachel Farmer**, working for a Grimsby fish merchant and later as a consultant, discovers hospitable patches on the newly-capitalist Russian landscape. She also manages to meet her literary heroes.

Even at official levels, there was more openness, a greater willingness to embrace Western and global standards where they were judged to improve current practices. **Marion Bates**, a psychologist, was able to secure a posting to the Moscow Police homicide department to help profile serious crimes. She, in effect, exports UK criminological techniques to Moscow and succeeds in winning over hardened Russian detectives.

Part III – Fissures and fireworks

The changing of the guard and break-up of the Eastern lands did not just have economic and cultural consequences. It also exposed old divisions, rivalries and prejudices. For a time it looked as if state-sponsored violence had merely been exchanged for ethnic violence. As a military interpreter in Bosnia, **Rod Thornton** sees horrors at first hand. He is part of a British army contingent sent to protect fuel supplies in Bosnia. As the mission expands, Thornton's small band is caught up in dangerous political games.

Vanessa Pupavac, visiting Bosnia to research nationalism, inadvertently inserts herself into one of the most vicious fratricidal wars that Europe has ever witnessed. In an unbearably tense journey, Pupavac and her fellow passengers witness more of the Bosnian war than they bargain for.

Finally, in this part, **Colin Davison**, a former journalist and expert observer of the East European media, notes that the seeds of violence never shrivel. Medieval and tribal ways of existence are always likely to return. His story reveals the ancient practice of vendetta in Yugoslavia, where never-ending cycles of murder trapped hundreds of families in misery.

Part IV – Resistance to change persists

Despite the changes to much of the social and physical construct of the former USSR and Eastern Europe, and the growth of conspicuous consumption in its western cities, old attitudes die hard. **Hannah Collins** lived for a year with an elderly widow in St Petersburg and found that the older generation was not entirely ready or happy to embrace the new order.

Through **John Butler**, who wandered for years in Russia and found solace in the Russian Orthodox faith, we are reminded of the distinctiveness of Russia's identity – a national character and spirit which is unchanging and which sets it apart from the global community of which it has never felt itself a member. His reflections of his time in remote Solovki, the scene of the Communist régime's worst excesses against the Church, are heart-rending.

Finally in this part, a chance trip to Russia to play mini-rugby led **Daniel Kearvell** into a decade of immersion and work in post-Soviet culture. Breakfast with cognac over business meetings in Archangelsk became the norm. But despite marrying a Russian, he accepts he will always be seen as an outsider in a society which still talks about 'us' and 'them'.

Part V – Life-long addicts

It is uncommon to find Western graduates who have lived or worked the Soviet Union and Eastern Europe throughout long periods of the post-Stalinist period. But they do exist and they provide a unique perspective on the region. One of these is **Keith Watkinson**, who from the 1950s onwards criss-crossed the Eastern bloc to promote British science and technology. His early experiences show that foreigners found it virtually impossible to do business of any kind in the USSR of the immediate post-Stalinist era. Years of hauling his young family from one end of the Eastern bloc to the other were exhausting, but frequently fruitful. And the hospitality he received was never less than entertaining.

The last narrative is provided by musician John Culley, who conducted a 40-year love-hate affair with Russia, including leading a tour of the country with a youth orchestra and acting as a guide in the 1980 Moscow Olympics. His narrative paints a colourful picture of the social and cultural evolution that took place in the former USSR.

The richness of the stories in this book, combined with their humour and candour, meant they were a joy to edit. At times the narratives are sad, but they are also unfailingly inspirational. Most are instructional too, grafting meat to the bare bones of well-known historical events or cultural shifts.

I hope and trust you will enjoy them as much as I did.

Phil Davis
September 2013

Phil Davis is a journalist, specialising in financial services. He was employed by the Financial Times *from 1998 to 2006 and has since worked as an independent journalist. While he still writes regularly for the* Financial Times, *he also advises investment firms on communications and investment strategy. In addition, he writes speeches for political and business figures and has authored a number of white papers on investment issues. He sometimes wishes he could have made better use of the BA in Russian and French he was awarded from the University of Nottingham in 1991, but will settle for having interviewed a couple of oligarchs in their native tongue.*

Inside the bell jar

In echoes of George Orwell's Nineteen Eighty-Four, **Jonathan Bastable's** *KGB case officers treated him as a friend, even a confidant. But Bastable was never a spy, so why did the KGB take such a close interest in him?*

The KGB was a security agency of the Soviet Union from 1954 to 1991. It was instrumental in crushing the Hungarian Revolution of 1956 and the Prague Spring of 1968. Its forerunner, the NKVD, conducted mass extrajudicial executions, ran the Gulag system of labour camps, suppressed underground resistance and conducted mass deportations to unpopulated regions of the country. Untold numbers of people were sent to Gulags and hundreds of thousands were executed by the NKVD.

ONLY once in my life have I been arrested. It was in Russia, in the summer of 1987, and I was working as a guide for Progressive Tours, the pro-Soviet travel agency that was then one of very few providers of study courses in the USSR. I was in charge of a group of British students who were doing a month's intensive Russian in the godforsaken town of Kalinin (now, as before the Revolution, Tver). One weekend, when there was nothing in the programme but a tiresome 'friendship evening' at a Palace of Culture, I took the chance to sneak off to Moscow to see my Russian friends. I clocked the uniformed policeman on the station platform, but told myself that there was no way that he was there for me. I got on the train and sat quietly in second class, looking forward to an evening of cold beer, *zakuski* (snacks) and conversation. But about 40 minutes into the journey I saw the policeman making his way down the carriage. I caught his eye and knew at once the game was up. He stopped in front of me. '*Dokumenty,*' he said laconically. There was an audible gasp from my fellow passengers when I produced a big, black British passport from the pocket of my coat. '*Nu i nu, popalsia,*' someone said. 'Well, well – that's *him* caught.' 'Come with me,' said the policeman, with a kind smile. 'Where to?' I asked. 'Back to Kalinin.'

We got off the train, which was about to stop anyway, and crossed to the other platform. 'I knew you were my man, as soon as I saw you at the station,' said the policeman, pleased with his professional eye. 'Why didn't you arrest me straight away, then?' I asked. 'I haven't officially arrested you,' he said – and he was adamant on that point. 'And anyway, you hadn't done anything yet. You didn't break the visa regime until you left Kalinin,' he added.

'I was going to Moscow, and my visa specifies both Kalinin and Moscow,' I said – though I knew the official response to that argument. The policeman supplied it: 'You are allowed to travel in a 40 kilometre radius of Kalinin, and a 40 kilometre radius of Moscow. Those two circles do not overlap. To get from Kalinin to Moscow you have to travel on a stretch of railway where you have no permission to be. That is where you were when I came and found you on the train.'

We arrived back at Kalinin station, where there was a small police office. 'This is where I leave you,' said the policeman. '*Ne obizhaisia,* don't hold it against me,' were his parting words. Two higher-ranking policemen sat behind a desk in the dimly-lit *punkt*. It smelled of Balkan tobacco and habitual tedium. 'Sit down, sit down,' one of them said, as if I had just arrived in his front room. Then, in a low whisper, he said to his colleague: 'What's the number?' 'What number?' '*Komitet*, the committee,' said the first, lowering his voice a little more.

My heart sank. He thought I wouldn't know what the committee was, but I had spent enough time with refuseniks and other *antisovietchiki* to know the shorthand. He was putting a call in to the Committee of State Security, the KGB. 'He's here,' said the officer joyfully to the person on the other end of the phone. It was as if he was phoning his wife to say that a long-awaited guest had arrived at his birthday party. 'Yes, it's him, Jonathan Swift...', and he laughed at his literary joke. He listened intently for his instructions, nodding from time to time, then put the phone down. He scrabbled around for a sheet of paper and a pen and came over to me. 'Jonathan, Jonathan... in Russia that's a kind of apple!' he beamed. 'Anyway, just jot down here what you were up to, why you were going to Moscow, names and addresses of anyone you were planning to meet up with – that sort of thing. As soon as you have done that, we can let you go.' I knew that the names and addresses were what the KGB wanted, and so were exactly what I should avoid writing down. Instead I wrote a terse defence of my actions: my visa specifies Moscow, and Moscow is where I was going. I declared myself astonished that this constituted any kind of police matter.

I was expecting someone from the KGB to turn up and take me elsewhere – but no-one came. Instead, the jolly policeman at the station let me sit with my statement for a couple of hours before putting in another call to the KGB. 'Jonathan's still with us!' he said, as though it had taken all his personal charm to persuade me to stick around. He listened again, said the odd '*Da...da...*' (Yes, yes...), then put the phone down. He came over and took my two-sentence statement. He glanced at it, but didn't seem in the slightest bit disappointed that I had not done as he had asked. 'You can go now,' he said. 'But straight back to the hotel, all right?'

There was a strange corollary to this episode. Our group had three Soviet tour guides, two young women and a man, all of them earnest, patriotic students of English. The man, Sasha, was the most serious of the three. He was working for the KGB. The day after my arrest, he approached me and said he needed a private word with me. We met later in the empty theatre of the pedagogical institute to which the group was attached. Sasha pulled up two chairs close to the stage. He cleared his throat nervously. The stage curtain was closed, and it suddenly occurred to me that someone might be sitting behind it, listening in. 'I know you are a good fellow, and I like you a lot,' he said. 'But I have heard what happened yesterday, and I am worried about it.' 'No need for you to worry,' I said breezily. 'It's all over now.' 'But I am worried about your future,' Sasha said. 'If it becomes known that you were arrested for breaking the laws of the USSR, that might make it difficult for you to find a job.'

I laughed, and this disconcerted Sasha. Clearly this was not the reaction he had been hoping for. '*Eto delo ser'eznoe*,' he said. 'This is a serious matter.' 'I'm sorry,' I said, still laughing. 'But if I were to tell anyone in England that you can be arrested in the Soviet Union for taking a train from one town to another, they wouldn't believe me. No-one would consider me a criminal. You have no need to worry on my behalf, Sasha. I promise you this won't affect my prospects at all.' The conversation continued for some time, Sasha constantly trying to get some leverage out of my arrest, to convince me that my entire career was on the line. It was clear that he had been coached for this conversation, that he had been given a line to take, and was lost for words once it didn't pay dividends at once. He looked defeated and unhappy when at last we left the empty theatre – like a man who had failed his driving test. I couldn't help feeling a bit sorry for him.

I was well acquainted with the KGB by then. I had spent a year in Leningrad as an undergraduate in 1982-83. I was then at Moscow University for almost two years in 1985-87. It was impossible to be a British citizen in the USSR in those days and not encounter the security police. In the earlier, pre-*glasnost'* period in particular, long-term westerners were few enough that every individual could be subject to surveillance. The watchers were not, in the first instance, burly men in trench coats, but the people one lived and socialised with: one's room-mates.

In Leningrad, each long-term western scholar shared a room in the hostel with a Soviet postgrad who, like Sasha in Kalinin, had been carefully screened and briefed beforehand. It was a prestigious thing for the Soviet students: if they passed muster, they got to live just two to a room (when four was the norm). More than that, they might get to enjoy or share in some of the riches that the westerners tended to bring in their wake: cassette tapes, peanut butter, foreign newspapers, hand-me-down jeans, tins of Heineken from a hard-currency 'Beriozka' shop...

But exposure to these things was seen as potentially corrupting, and for that reason only the most politically-sound students, Komosomol members with a long track-record of 'political literacy' were selected to live in Hostel No.2 on Shevchenko Street. Their prestigious billet came with an important civic duty: they had to file reports on their capitalist room-mates to the university's *otdel kadrov*, the personnel department. Everyone knew where their accounts went from there. Occasionally, the Soviet postgrad would have to attend the *otdel kadrov* in person, where two visitors from the 'organs' would ask questions about their roomie.

In short, every Russian who shared living space with a westerner was a *stukach* – a 'tapper' or KGB informer. That was the deal they signed up to. As with the *Stasi* in East Germany, it was ordinary citizens, regiments of politically-motivated gossips and eavesdroppers, who did the donkeywork of surveillance in the totalitarian state. In Hostel No.2 there were some Russians who had the decency to take their room-mates to one side and tell them about the banal Faustian pact that they had made. 'Don't tell me anything about where you go or who you see outside the hostel,' one Russian said to his British room-mate. 'I don't want to know anything about it.' Others relished the role, and saw it as a chance to shine. My room-mate, a preening communist called Vitaly, did his best to initiate political arguments, to elicit anti-Soviet remarks from me that he noted down and presented to his controllers like bouquets. 'How do the workers in Britain celebrate Lenin's birthday?' he once asked. 'They don't,' I said.

'Lenin's birthday is not a holiday in Britain – why would it be?' 'It may not be an official holiday,' he said. 'But all the working people take the day off anyway and march to the house where Lenin lived in London.' 'I doubt one in a hundred English workers know when Lenin's birthday is, or where he lived. He's Russia's hero, after all, not England's.' His face darkened; I had blasphemed. 'You are lying,' he said. 'All working people the world over know Lenin and honour his memory.' I shrugged, and he seemed to conclude that he had won the debate. I'm quite sure that is how he presented the exchange to the KGB – as a small rhetorical victory for socialism.

On another occasion, Vitaly initiated a discussion of the recent Falklands War. 'I don't understand why your Thatcher is sending her navy to the Malvinas,' he said. 'She has no right to act like a colonial conqueror; the British Empire is over now.' 'Maybe,' I said. 'But I don't understand how you can stand up for a fascist state when it invades a peaceful country. As a Russian, you should be ashamed of yourself.' That shut him up, and without my having to defend Mrs Thatcher; I was pleased with that. But I have no doubt that the conversation found its way onto my file in some form.

Some time ago I was approached by a publisher to write an article, provisionally entitled *The Pub Where Revealing Your True Name is a Deadly Mistake*. It was to be about a secret town called Gaczyna which, according to the brief, was a KGB training school hidden deep in Siberia. 'At Gaczyna,' read the brief, 'typical American and British towns were constructed as part of the training process. The American section had drugstores and motels, while the British section had traditional pubs. The trainee agents wore western clothes, spoke only in English, were known to each another only by western names...' I turned the job down, saying that I knew of no such institution, that the Polish rendering of the Russian place name was 'fishy', and that I very much doubted that anything like Gaczyna ever existed. Why would the KGB go to the vast trouble and expense of training people to pretend to act the part of Englishmen, when they had never had any difficulty finding real British citizens to work for them?

But I wasn't surprised that the publishing house thought it was for real. The KGB has always been seen in the West as secretive and all-knowing, but it was in fact neither. The KGB, at least the department charged with the surveillance of westerners, was (like the deluded Vitaly) almost comically ignorant of life in the countries that their targets hailed from. I was once interviewed by a KGB man at OVIR, the visa office on Kolpachny pereulok in Moscow, where I had to go every month to request permission to stay in the country for a few weeks more. Sitting in his dusty *kabinet* below a portrait of Felix Dzerzhinsky[1], the officer expressed astonishment that I, the son of a policeman, was allowed to leave Britain at all. 'My family can't go anywhere because of me,' he said. 'They are all *nevyezdnoi* – uncles, in-laws, nieces, all of them'. *Nevyezdnoi*: a succinct and almost untranslatable Soviet adjective that means 'forbidden for good or bad political reasons to travel beyond the borders of the USSR': unabroadable. The same man was amazed when I told him that higher education was free in Britain (those were the days). '*Nado zhe*', he said, over and over again. 'Well, I never.'

As for its activities inside Soviet borders, the KGB was not so much the secret police as the blindingly obvious police. Not for nothing was (is) the Lubianka, the headquarters of the KGB, a vast and extremely prominent building in the centre of Moscow. In every Soviet city, the KGB building was as conspicuous as a lighthouse on a clifftop. The security police did not work in the shadows: they wanted you to know that they had an eye on you – on you and everyone you knew. When I was at Moscow University in 1985-7, my room was turned over several times by the KGB. They always left a cigarette butt in the toilet as a kind of a calling card. This was standard practice. A friend who came from England to visit had his room in the Rossiya Hotel

---

[1] Founder of the Soviet Security forces, which later became the KGB

searched: he knew they'd been because they took the batteries out of his electronic chess set and kidnapped the white queen, scattering the other pieces on the floor.

The KGB took a close interest in me in those years – at first, I think, because I was a repetitive presence in the British contingent. Under the auspices of the British Council (BC) I spent a year in Leningrad as an undergraduate; after taking my degree I re-applied to the BC, and went to Moscow as a postgrad. I was preparing to write a thesis on the poetry of Akhmatova and Annensky – whose work I still love above everything in the Russian canon – but I was becoming ever more distracted and fascinated by the bloated, moribund monster that was the USSR. I wanted to explore and understand its unspoken rules, its arcane ways. I wanted to figure out how people operate inside a dictatorship, how they create a bubble of liberty around themselves inside which to breathe and think. The KGB was right to think that I was not quite what I was claiming to be, and that is why I found myself *pod kolpakom*, as the expression went: 'inside the bell jar', where they could keep an eye on me.

One day there was a knock on the door of my monkish block in MGU. This was not unusual in itself; I regularly had uninvited callers. Sometimes it was one of the *stukachi* (informers) assigned to the British contingent, wanting to have a chat and (if he was lucky) blag an embassy-bought custard cream. Other times it was a complete stranger, asking if I was the English guy with the guitar, and if so would I like to bring it to a birthday on the fifteenth floor. I had lots of enjoyable evenings and made many friends this way, banging out a couple of Elvis Costello party-pieces over vodka and *buterbrody* (open sandwiches), then passing the guitar on to the next strummer. I had an East German acquaintance who was a regular at these get-togethers. He always begged me not to acknowledge him in the corridors – not a nod or even a wink – if he was with one of his compatriots. 'They are nearly all Stasi,' he said. 'All the Germans are watching each other.'

This time the visitor was not someone I knew. He said his name was Valera and he was a friend of one the British teachers. I knew the teacher he meant; he had left the country rather suddenly and mysteriously some weeks before. Valera, who seemed troubled and jittery, said they had been close and he just wanted to know what had become of his English friend. I asked him how he got past the police check at the gate (he was not a student), how he knew where to find a Brit inside the immense rabbit warren of the Moscow University building. He waved this question aside and asked if I would have a drink with him outside one day soon. I told him I knew nothing whatsoever about why his friend had left so abruptly, but he implored me to meet him. I said I would.

Valera was gay – though he didn't come out and say so. When we met in town, he took me to a café, just behind the Bolshoi Theatre. In an underground way, this place was known to be Moscow's only gay bar – not that you would have been able to tell from the clientele that afternoon: the café was empty apart from two middle-aged women having a pre-theatre snack. Valera ordered a bottle of 'Soviet champagne' and when it turned out to be a dry *brut* he loaded his narrow glass with two teaspoons of sugar and stirred it vigorously with the wrong end of a teaspoon until the sugar had dissolved and all the bubbles had disappeared. As we worked our way through the bottle and then I think a second one, we had a strange and irksome conversation which consisted mostly of his insisting that I knew something I was not telling him, and my denying it. The talk became dull, and then irritating. I got up to go and tossed the money for the drink on the table. This imperious gesture seemed to wound him; unkindly, I had intended it to. 'Please don't,' he said softly – and I didn't know if he meant don't pay or don't leave.

It had been clear from the moment that he knocked on my door in MGU that that Valera was a *stukach*, albeit most likely an unwilling one. Homosexuality was still illegal and deeply shocking to the Russian sensibility, so perhaps he had been compromised in some way. I wasn't surprised when he called me a couple of days later and asked if we could meet up again – just to apologise. I wearily agreed. We met in the same place, outside the Bolshoi, and went to the same café, which was crowded that evening. But this time he brought along his 'cousin', a strikingly attractive young woman called Alla. She wore a brand-new Polish overcoat, vibrant red. I knew about that coat: there had been a shipment of them to Moscow a few weeks earlier and they had become a kind of one-garment fashion wave. You needed great contacts and plenty of roubles to get hold of one. The conversation followed much the same tack as our previous one, with Valera making the same veiled assertions in an ever more bad-tempered way. Only this time he would occasionally absent himself to say hello to people at other tables. This left me to talk to the charming Alla, who professed herself baffled by cousin Valera's bad-tempered behaviour and very sorry about the hard time that he was giving me.

In short, the whole thing was a set-up. Valera was sent to me to see if I might be gay – sometimes a default assumption of the KGB vis-à-vis English subjects. Alla was sent along to the second meeting to test the reverse assumption. I think, after this, the KGB decided it might be worth finding out a bit more about me, that I might be useful to them.

They began by hauling my Russian girlfriend out of class – as publicly as possible – and interviewing her. She was at Markhi, the Moscow Architectural Institute, which had a reputation for being a little too hippyish, somewhat subversive. The KGB didn't trust Markhi, where almost everyone was ironical about their *Komsomol*[2] membership, more interested in Lennon than Lenin. Markhi students joked that there was good reason that their college – and the equally dubious Stroganovka art school – were the two closest institutes to the Lubianka. Armed with a pair of opera glasses, it was said, the KGB could watch them without leaving their own office.

The friends of mine who were summoned to the *otdel kadrov* were all given the same spiel. First, they were asked

---

[2] Communist League of Youth.

generally about 'contacts with foreigners', then the questions homed in on me personally. 'We think he is working for British intelligence,' they said outright, citing the fact that I kept coming back to the country, that I did not seem to be an enthusiastic academic, that I had little to do with the other British students and that I had in the past expressed anti-Soviet opinions (fragments of ancient conversations with Vitaly and others were mentioned). 'If he's not a spy yet, he will be,' they said. This was wrong, but uncharacteristically astute. Before I went to Leningrad in '82, my father, then a chief inspector in the City of London Police, was approached by someone from Special Branch. My father's contact said they had heard that one of his boys was going to Russia and they were wondering if I might like to talk to them, maybe with a view to a career when I got back. 'With your Russian, you'd go far in Special Branch,' my dad said, adding doubtfully, 'if you are interested in that kind of thing.' I told my dad that I really wasn't and no more was said about it.

My case controller in Moscow, the officer who lightly interrogated my architect friends, passed a message to me via one of them that he would like to meet me in person. This felt serious. I was inclined to acquiesce, because I wanted to take the pressure off my Russian acquaintances. Also, I was about to re-apply for six more months at Moscow University; a refusal to meet might mean that my application was blocked. If, on the other hand, I showed willing and assured them I had no hidden motives, that might smooth my way back to Moscow. But it was obviously risky and compromising; I was in danger of getting drawn into a maze of subterfuge and *kompromat*.

I met my KGB man at the entrance to the Moskva Hotel on Prospekt Marksa. I saw him coming from the direction of the Lubianka. He was wearing a crumpled grey suit and tattered Romanian loafers. He introduced himself – Mikhail Vasilievich – and escorted me inside. We rode the lift to an unoccupied room, where he offered me a low armchair. He sat on a hard chair opposite me, looking down on me. I surreptitiously scanned the room for hidden cameras, but even though I could see none, I daresay the whole encounter was recorded. It felt a bit like a job interview but, bizarrely, it was as if Mikhail was trying to sell himself to me rather than the other way around. He never once referred to the KGB by name and when I did he winced as if I had committed some kind of *faux pas*. He said that our meeting was not in any way official, that I should look on him as one of my many Russian friends, that he was merely interested in the same things any friend would be: what life was like in a British university, what I thought about world affairs. At one point he said that he would be particularly interested in talking to me about my lecturers and professors, people I knew in the academic community.

Mikhail mentioned the British Embassy, a frown of distaste crossing his face as he did so. He said that there was no need to let anyone there know about our little chat. I said that I never went near the Embassy, which was true, and I mentioned in passing that the diplomats and the students did not get on all that well, partly because the former tended to be Thatcherite and pro-Establishment, while the latter tended to be left-wing and vaguely radical. There was a tradition that all the long-term students in the USSR were invited to come at Christmas to Moscow, where they were distributed to diplomats' families for a festive lunch. I told Mikhail that we had heard the dips refer to this as the 'descent of the great unwashed'. He was clearly fascinated to hear that there was any difference in outlook between the two main contingents of Brits in the country. I think that was the only useful piece of intelligence I gave him. He brought up my recent application to work as a translator for Progress Publishers. 'I can put in a good word for you if you like,' he said. 'It's no trouble.' I said no thanks – I'd rather get the work on my own merits. I later heard that he was struck by my refusal of his offer of help, even though it was a professional gambit designed to place me under an obligation. 'A lot of people are not so honourable,' he said to my girlfriend during a subsequent interview. 'Most are only too happy to grab a chance to get ahead.'

We had agreed in advance that the rendezvous would be a one-off, just a way to clear up a few points. I had made that an absolute condition of our meeting. But soon after that meeting in the Moskva, Mikhail took to calling me direct at the university, saying it was time we got together again. He began putting pressure on my Russian friends once more, who, unlike me, could not refuse to see him. So I agreed to a second rendezvous, same place. When I arrived at the street entrance to the Moskva, there was a black *chaika*[3] parked at the roadside – back door open, engine running, driver sitting rigidly with his eyes on the wheel. A beefy, overweight agent – the very caricature of a secret policeman – was patrolling the pavement, strolling up and down the section of pavement 100 yards either side of the hotel entrance where I stood. I made a point of looking him in the face each time he passed, but I never caught his eye.

Mikhail emerged from the hotel, about ten minutes after the appointed hour. He can only have been watching and waiting to see if I stuck it out, if the purring car and the menacing walker would scare me. 'Jonathan, let's go inside and talk,' he said. I didn't move from the spot. 'I just came to say I will not be meeting you again,' I said. 'I think we have said everything we need to say.' He tried hard to persuade me. 'It's very easy to make a mistake,' he said. 'Sometimes people make mistakes that they regret for the rest of their lives.' I fully expected the fat stroller to come up behind me, grab me by the shoulders and bundle me into the back of that *chaika*. Something along those lines had happened to an American journalist a few months before.

But thankfully no. We parted company on the street, and I never saw Mikhail Vasilievich again. Unlike the man from the Special Branch, however, he didn't just leave things be. He called from time to time – to congratulate me on New Year, or to ask if I'd like to go with him to the café at the top of Ostankino TV tower. 'It's a lovely afternoon out,' he said. 'And I just happen to have got hold of some tickets for...' I think Mikhail

---

[3] A model often used by Russian officials

Vasilievich had sold me to his superiors as a good prospect, a worthwhile lead. He was trying hard to make me pay dividends, to justify the faith that he had put in me. I was beginning to look like a professional failure for him. So when I left Moscow later that year, I thought my time in Russia was over forever, that I would not be allowed back, that exclusion would be the price of disappointing the KGB. I was delighted and surprised when later that year I was granted a visa to lead that group in Kalinin. The episode with the arrest on the train was, I now think, a last-gasp, slightly half-hearted attempt to make something of the investment of the KGB's time and effort – their Parthian shot in my direction. I suspect that after Sasha's clumsy approach they finally decided that I was, to use the official jargon, *neperspektivny*, terminally lacking in development potential.

At any rate, they left me entirely in peace when I went back in 1988. I got a small job as a fixer and translator for the correspondent of the *Wall Street Journal*. Those were exciting times, the dizzy, hopeful height of *glasnost'* and *perestroika*. One special highlight was meeting Roy Medvedev, the free-thinking Marxist historian. My American boss was to interview him at his flat and I went along to interpret. Medvedev was one of my heroes, someone who had fought hard against the system to speak the truth about Russia's past. He was making the most of the new historical sources that *glasnost'* had made available. When I met him he was writing two books on two separate typewriters, one in each room of his tiny flat. He would do a bit of work on one book, then wander into the other space and write a paragraph or two of the other. I found that deeply impressive.

When I returned at last to London, I started writing my own articles about the Soviet Union, and that eventually landed me a job on the *Sunday Times Magazine*. After the failed coup against Gorbachev in 1991, the editor of the newspaper, Andrew Neil, decided that coverage of Russia should be upped so I was transferred to the foreign desk and sent out to Moscow as 'Russian affairs correspondent'. The turbulent Yeltsin years had begun, a great time to be a reporter in Russia. Yeltsin himself was a large part of the story: bad-tempered, indecisive, increasingly slapstick. Once, after Gorbachev had given an interview critical of the government, Yeltsin in a fit of pique sent the police to close down Gorbachev's think-tank. I drove out to Gorbachev's HQ on Leningradskoe shosse to do a piece. Gorbachev stood on the street outside the sealed door of his HQ, speaking with great good humour to a huddle of journalists. He was one of those politicians – I have heard that Bill Clinton is another – whose physical presence is almost hypnotic. As he chatted away in his soft southern burr, I stood there marvelling at the fabulous clarity of his complexion. This is a man, I found myself thinking, who eats a lot of imported bananas. Gorbachev pointed to the KGB spooks watching him from across the road and we all agreed that they were a silly anachronism in the new, proto-democratic Russia; that it was absurd, in Moscow in the 1990s, for an ex-president to be acting the role of an old-time dissident.

The KGB, meanwhile, had reacted to the changing times by attempting to put on a human face. They took to releasing archive material about famous individuals that they themselves had repressed or liquidated, as if they had merely been stewarding this fascinating information until the time was right. Details emerged about the last days of writers such as Mandelstam and Babel; sometimes, entire unpublished manuscripts emerged from the stacks of shoeboxes in the Lubianka basement. The KGB set up a public relations department and even appointed a press officer, a tall Georgian fellow with a ready smile and a political handshake. Numerous former KGB officers, many of them having seen the light and renounced the organisation, became media pundits, the go-to guys for any western correspondent with a spy-themed story to stand up. The most personable of these freelance ex-*kagebeshniki* was General Oleg Kalugin, who wrote several racy books about his career as a spy in the US and elsewhere. He was nearest thing I ever encountered to a Gaczyna graduate: he spoke faultless English in a kind of aristocratic drawl, wore tweedy jackets and striped ties, and was an all-round Anglophile. In one of his books he mentioned that in the 1970s he was present at a meeting in KGB headquarters, where the problem of Georgi Markov was discussed. Markov, a Bulgarian dissident, was murdered in 1978. He was stabbed with an umbrella that had a poisoned tip – the KGB's idea of a perfectly camouflaged, culturally invisible weapon. When Kalugin made a routine visit to London after his book came out, he was arrested at the airport and questioned about Markov. I saw him in Moscow some time after and he was still upset about it. He would have been happy to chat to the chaps at the Met about anything; but to have his collar felt at Heathrow was so discourteous, so unnecessary, so un-British.

The KGB's PR department succeeded for a time in creating the impression that it was an entirely transparent organisation, that its doors were open to anyone. My editor in London once came to me with a great idea – why not wander over to the KGB archive and get Maggie Thatcher's file out? That would make a great story for Sunday. No such thing was possible, of course. The KGB never came close to opening the archives, or even allowing citizens to see their own files – as was the case in the former East Germany and elsewhere in eastern Europe. Unlike the Stasi, the KGB had not been disbanded. It was alive and kicking and institutionally resistant to reform. The biggest change at the Lubianka was a cosmetic one, the adoption of a new three-letter acronym: FSB.

In other former socialist countries, such as the Czech Republic, former members of the security services were banned from holding public office – a thoroughly sound policy. In Russia, meanwhile, the security organs were assiduously infiltrating the new political and economic structures. In the commercial sphere, many former officers set up companies that monetised their KGB background and training. (As an aside, one thing that troubled me about the Alexander Litvinenko affair was this: why was a dissenting former KGB officer in London, a voluble critic of the Putin regime, meeting up with serving FSB officers to discuss a business venture? '*Kto kogo*', as Lenin once said. 'Who was using whom?') In the political arena, the KGB/FSB seeped indelibly into the fabric of government, like black ink spilled on a bright new tricolour flag. Yeltsin in his latter years surrounded himself with *siloviki*, strongmen with roots in the security services. To his shame, he allowed them to affect his policy-making, to blunt his democratic edge. It is no secret that one of those advisers was Vladimir Putin. When Yeltsin named Putin as his heir apparent, I couldn't help remembering how distressed my acquaintances in Leningrad had been on the day that Yuri Andropov, the head of the KGB, succeeded Brezhnev. A KGB man in the Kremlin seemed a sickening, depressing prospect. Those friends would have been appalled to know that, 30 years on, the KGB and its heirs would again be in power, though the USSR itself was history.

When I look back on my own association with Russia over those same 30 years, my feelings are mostly happy ones: undying affection for people and places; a very Russian *toska*, that sweetly regretful longing for the days and the byways of youth; a genuine sense of privilege to have been close to history once or twice along the way; a gratitude for my knowledge of the Russian language and its literature, which have enriched my life in many ways. But when I look at Russia's present, the emotions are less positive, mostly a choking sense of disappointment that so many chances to take a better path have been missed. I am fearful, and I find it increasingly hard to summon up any gleam of hope, anything that feels like optimism for Russia's future.

Jonathan Bastable was at Nottingham (1980-84) including a year at Leningrad University. After graduation he went to Moscow to study the Acmeist poets, but was distracted by the political changes and was offered a job at The Sunday Times. *He later returned to Moscow; back in England worked as an editor in a publishing house, then became a freelance author. He is the author of a novel about the ill-fated Cathedral of Christ the Saviour.*

Games about frontiers

Behind the sabre-rattling and the rhetoric, the Cold War was played out in endless rounds of tit-for-tat expulsions and spygames. Diplomat and British Council Director **Terry Sandell** *became an unwitting participant and met Putin, Wilson and Thatcher in the process*

The Cold War, or the New Great Game, lasted from 1947 to 1991. It was so called because it did not feature direct military action, principally because both sides possessed nuclear weapons whose use would have guaranteed mutual assured destruction. Probably the most acute phases of the Cold war were the Berlin Blockade (1948–1949), the Korean War (1950–1953), the Suez Crisis and Hungarian uprising (1956), the Cuban Missile Crisis (1962) and the Vietnam War (1959–75).

It was my second job at the British Council and I was in London as Desk Officer for the Soviet Union and Mongolia. Until the late 1980s, there were really only two ways of visiting the Soviet Union professionally, via Communist Party/fellow-traveller channels or under the intergovernmental Anglo-Soviet Cultural Agreement exchange programmes, nearly all of which I managed on a day-to-day basis.

The programmes were often a mild part of a Cold War game, where visas would be refused, and horse-trading sometimes reached degrees of absurdity, with, say, a British scholar who wanted to carry out a comparative study of the relative clause in Georgian and Abkhaz having to be 'swapped' for a Soviet 'scholar' being sent to study at Porton Down. Even at the time, a lot of the logic of higher British policy in terms of relations with the Soviet Union escaped me. While on the Soviet side they wanted as restricted and controlled contact as possible, we theoretically took the opposite stance. The problem was that when there was a political crisis, as happened with the Soviet invasion of Afghanistan, we gave them exactly what they wanted by cutting back on exchanges and activity. Surely, I naively thought, we should have doubled the activity at such times?

As a result of the Helsinki Process the Soviet side had been forced to accept a couple of clauses in the Anglo-Soviet Cultural Agreement which allowed a very small number of direct invitations. That is, theoretically someone could be invited who had not been chosen/nominated by the 'sending side'. The Soviet authorities never used this clause since British people were not prevented from taking up invitations to travel to the Soviet Union, nor anywhere else. On the British side, we issued invitations, but it was only always after a great fight that some Soviet invitees were eventually allowed to come to the UK.

They were, however, often significant visits. One brought Alfred Schnittke and introduced his music to British audiences, but only after a last-minute showdown when the Soviet authorities threatened to stop the visit. They only backed down when we warned that the live concert of his music to be broadcast by the BBC to coincide with the visit would be accompanied by a full explanation of why he could not be present.

Another memorable visit of this type, but for different reasons, was that of the Director of the Moscow Zoo. His visit was such a professional success that he decided he wanted to present a thank-you gift to Britain and suggested pelicans for St James's Park (just across the road from both the British Council HQ and the Foreign Office). After clearing everything with the Royal Parks administration the proposed gift was accepted. With Anglo-Soviet relations so dire, I felt this was a golden opportunity to portray a positive and human dimension to the difficult relationship, as well as to exploit an unmissable PR opportunity. The pelicans duly arrived and received considerable positive publicity. Unfortunately, however, they received even greater publicity when it was discovered that some of the bird-life in St James's Park was being mysteriously found dead. It turned out that the culprits were the Soviet pelicans and this provided some splendid Cold War journalistic copy. The pelicans, *personae non gratae*, soon found themselves behind bars in a zoo.

In the summer of 1979, I worked in the Cultural Section of the British Embassy in Moscow on secondment to the Foreign Office as acting Cultural Attaché and covering leave absences. This led in 1981 to a substantive secondment and posting when the Cold War was in full swing. Most staff in the Embassy were discouraged or forbidden from mixing with Soviet people, but certain Embassy roles required contact and travel, and I was lucky in that respect. As with many features of life in the Soviet Union, there were paradoxes. A British diplomat casually meeting and talking to a student on a train would have been anathema to the Soviet authorities and it could have been potentially damaging to the student's career or family. There was not, however, normally a problem meeting senior people if one went through the right channels and as a result I could socialise with leading cultural figures. In spite of the restrictions, I was able to meet, for example, poets such as Yevtushenko, Voznesensky, Akhmadulina. For all the negative aspects of being monitored in Moscow by the KGB, constantly being followed in other cities one visited and never being able really to unwind or lower one's guard, there were many such positive experiences.

The constant surveillance was, however, often intrusive. I think the only time I relaxed during the period in Moscow was one New Year's Eve when we decided to go to Red Square with some Soviet 'champagne' to join the crowds and see in the

New Year. On returning home, we discovered that our flat, in a closely-guarded foreigners' compound with reasonably serious locks provided by the British Embassy, had been entered and our extensive collection of records had been strewn about the floor with some cigarette ends stamped on some of the discs. Such incidents were sometimes termed 'visits from the Gas Board', as on more than one occasion when caught red-handed in foreigners' flats, the perpetrators claimed they were reading the gas meters.

The diplomatic expulsion game was, of course, a prominent feature of the Cold War. It only touched me once and briefly. From a period of research in Edinburgh, I had become interested in the history of ideas in the eighteenth century and met a Russian specialist who was working on the history of science in the eighteenth century. He offered to give me a copy of his paper on it. We met in a small park near the Embassy on a cold winter's day, chatted for a short time and then he opened his briefcase and handed me the paper. Some days later the Ambassador was called to the Ministry of Foreign Affairs and was informed that I had been receiving secret documents and they produced photographs to 'prove' it. They hinted at expulsion but in fact nothing happened. It is probably relevant that the Russian specialist was Jewish and had been applying for emigration.

There were other underlying tensions when working as a diplomat in Moscow at that time. Security was a major Embassy preoccupation, but while it was understandable and almost normal to hold meetings in a special floating chamber which prevented eavesdropping, there was also a rule to list the names of all Soviet citizens with whom one had had any contact whatsoever. This was fine for many in the Embassy as they rarely had such contacts, but my job involved a relatively large amount of time meeting people, so producing a comprehensive list was a great chore and I was not always as conscientious as the system demanded. Similarly I found the internal security checks on my waste-paper basket tiresome, especially as even a stray envelope could represent a breach (which happened once in my case) – and three breaches could mean the posting being terminated.

After Moscow, I moved to Vienna where I eventually became Director of the British Council. I was there for a very enjoyable five years. From Vienna I moved back to Moscow in early 1989 where I stayed until late 1992 and witnessed at first hand the collapse of the Soviet Union. I was initially seconded to the Foreign Office as Counsellor for Cultural and Educational Affairs in the Embassy. At this time there was a serious turf dispute between the Embassy and the British Council as to who should be in charge of cultural activity. The British Council saw my role exclusively in terms of turning the Cultural Section of the Embassy into a British Council operation. In those heady times things were moving so fast and there was so much activity that nobody could really keep up and I relatively soon moved what had become the British Council Section out of the Embassy 'fortress' into specially designed premises within the Library of Foreign Literature. With the superb and courageous staff of the Library we were able to develop very positive, mutually-beneficial co-operation and the creation of an independent British Council.

The aims of Gorbachev's reforms had been to reinvigorate communism and the Soviet Union, not to get rid of it. The new paradigm mutated, however, evoking Macmillan's explanation of the fall of a government: 'Events, dear boy, events.' Travelling widely within the Soviet Union in 1989 and 1990, I was uniquely positioned to feel what was happening, although it differed from place to place. Of the changes that had taken place, the most important one was that people's fear of intimidation or persecution by the authorities had by and large disappeared. This meant also that I was able to be in open contact with people whom I had known from my previous time in the Soviet Union. One of them, Lennart Meri, with whom I had collaborated in earlier times to get books and other materials to Estonia's leading university, Tartu, had undergone a real change. From being basically a dissident, he found himself the Estonian Minister of Foreign Affairs. I remember long conversations with him and being heavily influenced by his analysis of what was happening to the Soviet Union. Later, he became the first President of independent Estonia and we had a joyful reunion when I was one of a trio accompanying a Foreign Office Minister to the Baltic countries on a mission to recognise and celebrate their renewed sovereignty.

The collapse of the Soviet Union was there for all to see, but ironically even western Kremlinologists did not want to see it. There were various reasons for this. The first was that it was not only Soviet citizens who had been brainwashed or fooled by the empty boasts of the Communist Party and Soviet government machinery. A second reason was the unbelievably powerful influence Gorbachev personally wielded on Western policy-makers, who projected onto him what they wanted him to be rather than what he actually was. A third, and possibly the most powerful reason, was that virtually all the Western Soviet specialists were Russian-speaking, Russo-centric and often Russophile. Little serious analysis was available about the constituent parts of the Soviet Union with its myriad of nations, nationalities and once proud cultures, and there was little recognition of their re-emerging aspirations.

Travelling at this time all over the Soviet Union, I could see that while there were important local differences between Georgia and Estonia, Ukraine and Azerbaijan, Lithuania and Moldova and so on, the centre was no longer in total control and the regions were no longer in total fear. As the Soviet Union began to be reminiscent of the Emperor's New Clothes, what struck me most was that the collapse would come because of what had held it together. The simple truth was that the various Soviet republics had little or no direct relationship or horizontal cooperation with each other except through Moscow. Once Moscow collapsed, or became too preoccupied with itself, there was no glue holding the constituent parts of the Soviet Union together.

In 1990, I spent a lot of time in Kyiv working on a big British cultural festival. My interest in Ukraine had been long-standing and went back to research at Edinburgh University and an interest in the writer, Vasyl Kapnist. It was fascinating to see how the move to independence developed there 200 years after Kapnist. Kapnist, or his brother, had made a trip to Berlin in 1791 to seek Prussian support for a Ukrainian uprising against Russian imperial rule that had recently exported serfdom there and suppressed traditional local Ukrainian institutions and social structures. Again, people in the West either did not want to see or could not understand what was happening in Ukraine. I had to fiercely fight my own side to stop the design materials for the 1990 British Festival in Kyiv incorporating the hammer and sickle.

Even Mrs Thatcher seemed confused. She came to Kyiv for the festival, where we gave her a busy programme visiting events and meeting people. A vivid memory of her remains with me. I had been showing her around an exhibition and introducing her to local Ukrainians and as she left me to go to a car that was taking her to the Rada (the Ukrainian Parliament, which she was going to address), I noticed blood dribbling from her heels. I was told later that she always bought a new pair of shoes to go on foreign trips. Her speech to the Rada was very ambiguous in terms of the future of the Soviet Union and Ukraine and I mused later whether this lack of her usual clarity was because of her liking for 'doing business' with Mr Gorbachev or whether her excruciatingly painful feet may have dulled her vision.

One of the other people with whom I had had contact earlier in my career, and with whom I renewed relations, was a former academic from the Law Faculty of Leningrad University, Anatoly Sobchak. He now found himself Mayor of St Petersburg and was widely seen as a potential future president. Having set up an independent British Council operation in Moscow, the next stage was to set up offices or local operations in the republics which we did initially in the Baltic states, in Ukraine and Belarus. I also wanted to have a base in St Petersburg and so had regular meetings with Sobchak who had made it clear that he would do his best to help.

At the beginning we were usually on our own for the visits and they were as much social as official occasions with tea and splendid cakes in his office. Later, when the desire to set up a British Council office there had become a realistic possibility, he explained that it would be sensible if he invited one of his staff to be present at the meetings to do any follow-up work. The person Sobchak chose was the Head of the Foreign Relations Department, a short, slightly sullen man, who was not invited to join in on the tea and cakes but sat some way away taking occasional notes of our conversation. His name was Vladimir Putin.

Terry Sandell studied Russian at the University of Nottingham from 1967 to 1970. Currently Director, Cultural Futures LLP and a Senior Associate at St Antony's College, Oxford he is working on various cultural policy and development projects in the Russian Federation, Ukraine, Belarus, Moldova, Armenia, Azerbaijan and Georgia, and is writing a book on Ukraine. His earlier career included being a volunteer in Africa, a diplomat in Moscow, director of an international arts promotion agency and various British Council posts. He set up the British Council in the Soviet Union, becoming its first director. After ten years as Director of Visiting Arts, an organisation promoting international arts projects and networks, he re-joined British Council as director in Ukraine after the 'Orange Revolution'. Awarded an OBE for his contribution to Anglo-Russian relations, he also has an honorary doctorate from the Ukrainian Academy of Pedagogical Sciences.

The Wild East

Daniel Vowles *discovered that market reforms in the former Soviet Union did not mean that the streets were paved with gold*

Following the dissolution of the Soviet Union, President Boris Yeltsin promoted privatisation to spread ownership of former state enterprises (in order to create political support for his economic reforms). In late 1992, Yeltsin gave free vouchers to all citizens as a way to transfer ownership and give mass privatisation a jump-start. The shares ended up in the hands of a small group of tycoons in finance, industry, energy, telecommunications and the media who came to be known as oligarchs. By mid-1996, substantial ownership over major firms resided in the hands of these oligarchs, who notably included Boris Berezovsky, Vladimir Potanin, Mikhail Khodorkovsky and Vladimir Bogdanov. These individuals quickly asserted considerable power over the Russian economic and political landscape.

AFTER graduating in 1993, I wasn't too sure what I was going to do. All I knew was that it had to be related to Russian and to Russia. We had all had great business ideas while wandering around Moscow's Yugo-Zapadnaia looking for our daily *falafel* – such as the first British fish and chip shop. To no-one's surprise, somehow it never happened (maybe a good thing as we would probably be fish food now, given the influence of the Mafia in Moscow at that time).

So after six months of applications to all the big companies who weren't really – believe it or not – yet convinced of the potential of the Russian economy, I replied to an ad in the Nottingham graduate press which ran something like: 'Russian speaker who has all his life insurance policies in place wanted in very gloomy environment.' Never has an advert been so accurate. Anyway, I got the job and I was sent to the Ukrainian-Moldovan border.

God knows how, but within a few weeks I had gained responsibility for ensuring that the fruits and vegetables frozen in a Ukrainian canning factory run by the Chechen Mafia were of a high enough standard to be bartered for combine harvesters. (An American company was selling the combines to the factory which had no cash so they paid in vegetables, and our company was hired by the Americans to guarantee they didn't get paid with 500 tonnes of sludge). Thus, I was cast as the nasty enemy sent by Americans to control local interests. I was put up in the 'swish' hotel Smotrich, which had no hot water and, on days with the letter 'y' in them, very often no cold either. To add to this, there was no food in the building (not even for breakfast) and the lift didn't work. And yes, Room 705 meant the seventh floor.

On meeting the factory director, I was told that I was to be assigned Vasis as my driver (he did plenty of spying on me and very little driving) and was offered a choice of hand guns (politely refused) which 'may come in handy'. I was starting to think at this point that maybe I should have concentrated on the French part of my degree. Vasis's Lada had an unusual feature in the form of a gearstick that unscrewed and gave access to a machete.

I had arrived at Easter and of course all the shops were shut. Not a 'sausage' in town – how I was going to regret that word. The director's right-hand man had had a brand-new house built at the edge of the factory and I was told, rather than invited, to stay at his house 'permanently' rather than stay at the hotel where I could not be watched. For a few days I resisted, but a little light demolition of my hotel room while I was out one day persuaded me. Thankfully I had a strange premonition and previously hid my money under a floorboard. But, maybe it was for the best since there was no food around and at least I could get some here. I was taken to a million relatives of Vasis's over the next couple of days in the countryside and in each small wooden house was the same spread: home-made sausage, *salo* (it's just fat) and *samogon* (home-made vodka). Roll on Tuesday, when work resumed.

After the holiday weekend, the factory was alive again and they had a delivery of *kabachki* (turnips). I think it had been raining turnips all weekend: my meals were now taken in the factory and to my delight breakfast consisted of fried egg, with turnip, and lunch was turnip with turnip and dill leaf.

Fortunately help was at hand and someone far better experienced than me in the process of quality control arrived after a few weeks. Now, as there were two of us, we demanded a car and accommodation away from the factory grounds. Our wishes were granted. We got a Lada Niva, with three of the four cylinders working, and five litres of petrol a week. And we moved back to the hotel... Or so they thought. We actually hired a flat which we never actually slept in, but used for all meals and – most importantly – to make telephone calls. These were still the days of ordered calls at the post office and the average wait was three days.

We would return to the hotel to sleep, or rather to be spotted entering the hotel. We would get extra petrol on the black market and escape the town to escape the surveillance and go down to the lake, swimming and grilling food on a fire.

Now that the freezing products for the American contract were under the control of my colleague, I was asked by my UK company to find strawberries for exporting. So I hired a Kamaz truck and a driver, Nikolai, (obviously Vasis came too) and off we went through the Carpathian mountains. What an unforgettable experience: we travelled to every village and we would open the back of the Kamaz and produce weighing scales at each one. After a chat with the head of the village (who obviously took his cut) everyone in the village who had a bike started pedalling up to the lorry with all the strawberries they could carry. Talk about organic farming; it took a day to get three tonnes. I remember our evening meals in the Kamaz of sausages, *salo* and something rather hideous sealed in jam jars that was washed down with vodka.

Then our mission to get the strawberries back to the factory began. It had taken about three days to get the strawberries and there wasn't a lot of time left to save them before they turned to juice. Fate conspired against us. I couldn't believe it as we rolled into the canning factory... It was pitch black. Power cut. By morning it was too late. We tried to freeze them, but they had mashed together and the most enormous frozen strawberries the size of boulders came down the line. I have never laughed so much.

Then the situation started to change from comically bad, to really bad. We had the idea to make jam out of the giant strawberries and it turned out to be pretty good. I went to speak to the director about purchasing the final product on behalf of the UK company and he sent me off to the *planovaia* (production planning department) which dealt with this. Now we came to a 'sticky' problem – they had made the jam with *my* strawberries, but they still seemed to have those big red giants in the cost calculation. In other words, the director didn't just want to charge me for the production costs of using his factory, but also for the strawberries which I had sourced myself. We tried talking it out, but we just couldn't see eye to eye on it.

However, this disagreement was suddenly made to look insignificant. The quality of the frozen peas, which after all was the main reason we were there, was not up to standard and a big row was looming. We had sent comments back to the UK and suddenly everyone was called to Kiev for a meeting between the American purchasers of the veggies (the ones giving the director a few millions' worth of brand spanking new machinery), us quality controllers, and...yes, the director, Mr Mafioso himself.

As my time in Ukraine was supposed to be coming to an end (since it was the end of the vegetable season), I was glad to hear that I could go to this meeting and then on to the airport. So forgetting our strawberry differences for a while, I travelled with Mr Director in his chauffeur-driven four-wheel drive Land Cruiser to the meeting with the US company, who were a little worried about the quality of their frozen peas. Believe me, you need a lot of good quality peas to buy a combine harvester.

As we entered the office, I learned that my new colleague was not coming, but had sent his report for me to read aloud at the meeting. We all sat down and after a while the American client turned to me and asked for the report on the factory's performance and whether it was sufficient to enable the delivery of quality goods to exchange for their multi-million pound equipment. I had not read the report. I don't remember all the details, but it went approximately like this: 'The director is a complete cretin who has no chance of delivering the goods and the whole thing is going to be a disaster.'

I could feel the director's black eyes drilling a hole in my forehead. But, hey, I was off to the airport and back to UK in a few hours. However, there was a nightmarish conclusion to the meeting: 'Well it seems pretty bad, Dan, you had better go back to the factory and keep an eye out down there.' I couldn't believe they were asking me to go back to the factory. In a few hours I would find myself on the 'express' train leaving Kiev, but going south, not west. Funnily enough, there was no place for me in the Land Cruiser on the way back.

When we got back, Mr Big was not over-friendly. He quickly returned to the question of the strawberries and after long negotiations (of about 45 seconds) he told me to pay him or else. I was starting to think that my monthly wage of £670 was not worth this amount of hassle. My colleague and I decided that I should get out of town rather sharpish, which was rather generous of him. (He had managed to persuade Mr Big he was nothing to do with the UK company and thus could stay on and maintain the quality checks independently.)

So off I went to get a train ticket out of there... But to no avail. The ticket lady at the station refused point blank to sell me a ticket. I couldn't believe it. She stated that Mr Big had said I couldn't leave town. This was getting scary.

I had got to know Vasis, my driver, quite well over the previous few months and he agreed to drive me to Khmelnitsky, about an hour away, where I could surely purchase a train ticket. Khmelnitsky had a sort of police guard on its perimeter and as we approached they flagged us down. No, we were not allowed to pass. Factory Director says no.

The next day we tried again with the subtle difference that I was hidden on the Lada's rear floor under a blanket. I don't think my heart rate really slowed until I was on that train from Khmelnitsky to Kiev.

My next 'dream' posting was to Kaliningrad. I have to admit that even after studying Russian for five years at school and four years at university, I couldn't find Kaliningrad on the map. I found Kalinin, but no Kaliningrad. The reason is that Kaliningrad is separated from the rest of Russia by Lithuania and Belarus, so it's a bit like having the county of Somerset on the other side of Berlin. The Russians won't let it go and the unfortunate population that live there are rather cut off from everywhere. They can't leave Kaliningrad for Western Europe without a visa and to go anywhere else in Russia they need to take a plane.

The upside was that this created quite a few trading opportunities. My job, for the same UK company, was to try to interest the Kaliningrad shops in British products. For a month or so, I walked the streets of Kaliningrad compiling a list of the products that were missing from the marketplace, such as Cornflakes, Pedigree Chum and non-drip paint, to name a few I remember. I would discuss ideas with my Russian partner, ex-navy, now capitalist, who worked out of an office at the back of the almost derelict *Kaliningradvagonzavod* which, in better times, had been one of the Soviet Union's prime rolling stock manufacturers. We agreed on the products and asked the UK to send us a twenty-tonne lorry loaded with the selected goods.

After the delivery (two weeks later, by a rather neurotic non-Russian-speaking Suffolk driver) we had to devise a selling strategy. It was not always easy to persuade my Russian colleagues of the merits of these products. A lot of heated discussions took place about non-drip gloss, for example. I remember they held the pot upside down and tried to spread it on bits of old newspaper, accusing me of trying to sell them cottage cheese instead of paint. In the end I managed to convince them of the superior quality of the products and gained a little trust.

However, one little surprise was in store for me. My UK colleagues had informed me before the lorry left that they had added a few crates of jeans, as they had got a great discount on them. With my Russian business partner, we went to see the boss of the most exclusive jeans shop in the town. My partner told me that it wouldn't be easy to persuade him to take our jeans since he had contracts signed up with some rather unsavoury suppliers. To our surprise, the owner, Vladimir, decided to take a few pallets, saying that he wouldn't order from his other suppliers for a while. A week or so later, the lorry arrived and we started to unpack it in the warehouse.

An hour later I was wishing I was still in the pea factory in Ukraine. You have never seen so much rubbish in one place. The jeans came in all shapes and sizes, some with one leg, some with one and a half legs, some with one leg purple and the other blue, some with holes, some with threads hanging out. Although it was minus ten degrees, the temperature in the warehouse got rather hot. The shop owner, Vladimir, was impatiently waiting for his delivery so we spent a day or two sifting through it all trying to salvage enough stock to keep Vladimir happy. We finally went to see him with twenty or so pairs, telling him that the rest were still on the way from England. We sent the rest back.

The incompetence of my company then reached another high, as they messed up the papers and sent the consignment to Poland by mistake. And guess who had to go and rescue them?

Off I went and yet another adventure in the Wild East was about to begin.

Dan Vowles studied at Nottingham 1989-93. He visited Russia in 1990 and during a second stay heard Gorbachev announce that the Soviet Union had finally run its course. On graduating he worked for companies in Ukraine and Russia as their free market economies sluggishly emerged, and he now runs a hotel in northern Poland.

Military games and capitalist capers

Will Stamper *discovered the Soviet Union in the last days of the Cold War, was pitted against it, and finally learned to love it*

On August 13 1961, East Germany erected a barbed-wire barrier that would later be expanded through construction to create the Berlin Wall. Before the Wall's erection, 3.5 million East Germans defected from the German Democratic Republic. Between 1961 and 1989, the Wall prevented almost all emigration. During this period, around 5,000 people attempted to escape over the wall, of whom about 600 were killed. After weeks of civil unrest, the East German government announced on 9 November 1989 that GDR citizens could cross into West Germany. The Wall was destroyed in 1990, paving the way for German reunification.

Introduction: playing cat and mouse with the Soviet army

In the summer of 1990, I was serving in the British Military Mission (BRIXMIS) in Berlin as a 29-year-old army infantry captain in the Staffordshire Regiment conducting intelligence missions into the Soviet Zone of Germany, a post known within the Mission as a Tour Officer. The mission tour comprised a team of three, based at the British Berlin headquarters at the Olympic Stadium and we travelled in a Mercedes jeep or *Geländewagen*. The driver was an RAF or Army Corporal trained in evasive driving.

The second member was a senior NCO or warrant officer, often SAS, Parachute Regiment, Guards or RAF. One of his roles was to navigate and keep an eye on the RAF or Army officer, who was the Tour Officer. The tour officers all spoke Russian to interpreter level and were trained how to use a Nikon F3 camera as the main tool of their trade. No weapons, no radios.

We toured for around three days, leaving West Berlin to cross the Glienicke Bridge at Potsdam, the notorious place of spy exchanges at the height of the Cold War. Over the next few days, we drove hard and slept rough, engaging in a game of cat and mouse, where the mouse was trying to obtain photographs of Soviet military vehicle movements and the cat was trying to catch and detain them in the act of intelligence gathering. The same kind of procedure was being carried out daily in West Germany, by SOXMIS, our Soviet counterparts.

The Soviet army fuel bowsers had *ogneopasno* (flammable) painted on them and the tourers referred to these as 'oglypoglies'. The soldiers regulating Soviet army traffic convoys were known as 'reggies' (*regulirovshchiki*), the discovery of whom was joy for any tour crew as they knew a convoy was soon on the way and they just had to hide and wait and then 'run' them. We would set up a static observation point or our driver would drive at speed past the convoy, the warrant officer calling the vehicle or 'kit' description into a recorder and the officer would test the speed of the Nikon motor drive by snapping the vehicle registration numbers at up to six shots a second. This practice had been perfected over more than 40 years and was high adrenalin, high risk. Of all the mission commands, the one which jolted everyone into life – and to this day will make an ex-mission member leap – is: 'KIT!'

I arrived at the very end of the mission's 45 years of operations and conducted six of the final tours. On the last day before German reunification, most of the mission met for a final celebratory BBQ in uniform out in a field near Potsdam. In the evening, we invited the Soviet Army Liaison team to the Potsdam Mission house, a lovely, large detached residence in Potsdam. For the last time, we lowered the British Flag as the Last Post sounded from the roof

– it truly signalled the end of the Cold War. We then drove back in a long convoy across the Glienicke Bridge, met by hundreds of local Potsdam residents who, knowing the historical significance of the occasion, had lined the streets from the Mission House to the Bridge to wave us off. A deeply-moving occasion of mixed emotions. The Mission House was subsequently handed back to its original owner from before the Soviet occupation of Germany.

After the Mission ceased touring and before I was summoned to join the build-up to the 1990-91 Gulf War, I spent a month or so as an army liaison officer, working between the Soviets and the newly-appointed German *Bundespolizei* in an eastern region of the freshly-unified Berlin. The Soviets were due to have one of their November memorial parades, to mark their people's suffering at the hands of the Germans. I translated between a Soviet Colonel and a West Berlin policeman. The Soviet Colonel explained where the army trucks would gather and park as they always did to disgorge their parade soldiers. The *Bundespolizei* just said: '*Nein, nicht da.*' No, not there. The Colonel stared in disbelief, turned and walked away. The game was up.

In the Officers' Mess in Berlin at the same time, we planned a Russian night for British officers and wives. The next day I was leaving for Riyadh, via RAF Brize Norton. I planned the function and arranged the menu of *borshch, blinchiki, pelmeni* and so on, chose Russian music to dance to and we all dressed up. As my highly illegal guest of honour, I chose a huge Siberian bear of a Soviet Lieutenant, Dmitri from Novosibirsk, who was a member of the Soviet liaison team in Berlin. I had invited him informally, not knowing what risks he was taking, but he accepted informally and we somehow smuggled him past the gate sentry at the Berlin HQ barracks and welcomed, I suspect, the first unofficial guest Soviet Army officer to attend a British Army party. The evening was a wild success, we all drank masses of vodka, made lavish toasts to peace and danced on the Mess tables. The only hitch came at the end of the evening, when Dmitri was too drunk to go home and slept on the floor of my room in the Mess, spread-eagled around my army kit, which was all laid out to be packed for the Gulf the next day. I remember waking up in the morning, peeling my eyes open and staring across at his huge bulk, asleep on his back, snoring loudly and through my woodpecker headache I remember feeling elated at how the world had changed.

A rude initiation

The world in 1990 was considerably different to a decade earlier when I got my first taste of the Soviet Union. It was the summer of 1980 and these were my first few hours in the Soviet Union, a first-year student of Russian. I peered wearily out of the coach window onto the outskirts of Krasnodar; it was after midnight and hot and sticky. The coach had halted at an interchange of road and tram lines and work was going on under dull blue-grey street lights. We were a group of nearly 80 students from British universities, exiled to a month of Russian language study in Krasnodar instead of the usual venue Voronezh, which was off-limits due to the Moscow Olympics.

The images outside became clearer. There were shadowy silhouetted tram workers levering and lifting heavy tram rails, working as a cumbersome team. My brain flickered into life: 'My God, it's a woman'. Then I saw another and another; short, squat, solid women with headscarves and rough uniforms. And then came the stomach punch: 'They are all women!' What kind of a regime has night shifts entirely staffed by women struggling with enormous tram rails?

The month in Krasnodar created a mass of indelible impresssions, both positive and negative, but mostly shocking to a young British student with no idea of what to expect from the Soviet Union.

I was sponsored by the British Army while at Nottingham University and had received my Intelligence Corps security briefing on how to behave and what to avoid for my month inside the Soviet Union, but I still could not comprehend how differently such a vast population lived.

On arrival, we were placed three to a room on the top, eleventh, floor of the hall of residence of the foreign language institute. It was the Soviet summer vacation and the rest of the building was empty. Anxious questions flowed: Why the top floor? And why were we being looked after by a team of twelve young and inexperienced *Komsomol* students? Why were the showers so far away on the ground floor? Why was there no hot water upstairs? Why no toilet seats and no toilet paper? And why this endlessly terrible smell? I remember walking along the corridor, turning to look into rooms with groups of our girls huddled on the barrack beds, many already in tears. We were to live there for the next month. The first night felt like we had voluntarily entered some sort of god-forsaken prison. There was no way to call home; we were alone inside the Soviet Union.

Girls went to the showers in pairs, as towels and clothing had started to disappear from the changing rooms – one girl showers, the other guards. The canteen became famous for its 'deathburgers'. I befriended the lady who took the dirty dishes at the kitchen hatch, each day adding one more *spasibo* (thank you) to her reply of *pozhaluista* (don't mention it). The glass in her spectacles was badly cracked, but the humour and warmth of her eyes shone through.

One day I spotted a dead male body lying under a window near our hall of residence. I remember the shock of still seeing it there several hours later. One morning, I walked into the language institute past the *dezhurnaia* (hotel or hostel duty attendant) whistling. I was immediately reprimanded with: 'We don't whistle!' It apparently means that you will have no money, so I hereby offer a reward to anyone who can remember a local person whistling casually within the former Soviet Union.

We often played knock-about evening football among the students, British and locals together. We asked the Soviets if they wanted to play a match, just for fun – we did not really rate ourselves. Much to our surprise, a team from the local power station turned up in full kit and with a trainer. We were shocked and annoyed, as it seemed a political move to assert superiority over us, and a certain fighting spirit arose within and we came back from 1-0 down at halftime to win 2-1. It felt at the time like a massive human, political and international victory.

Our student group splintered into two factions, a few who objected to the UK government boycott of the 1980 Moscow Olympics and the rest of us, who decided to avoid an overt show of politics. The tensions were palpable – it was a time when political belief was writ larger than today.

Siberia starts to thaw

After the games of cat and mouse with the Soviet army, I returned to Russian lands to pursue what in theory would be a less high-octane job. It didn't necessarily turn out that way.

In 1992, just before the Gulf War, I met Zoe in Riyadh, a daughter of a British Aerospace executive, whose parents lived in Saudi Arabia, but who was born considerably to the north of Saudi, in Blackpool. I resigned my Army commission, we married and I landed a job in Irkutsk – as you do – half way across Siberia, on the shores of Lake Baikal. Zoe joined me in June 2002, with Muffin, her beloved English Cocker Spaniel. This was new and different. This was now Russia in 1992, with hyperinflation, massive unemployment and dollars trumping roubles. We lived there from 1992-93 and many strange things happened.

I was employed by a Russian-US joint venture to start up a timber mill for the processing of indigenous Siberian pine and larch for the Japanese construction market. The mill was near the banks of the River Angara, the only outlet from the massive Lake Baikal. When I arrived in February 1992, the fishermen selling freshly caught Omul fish on the banks of the Angara would accept only a half litre of vodka as payment for a kilogram of fish. When I left in June 1993, they would only accept USD, no vodka, no roubles. From high liquidity to hard currency.

Life was rough and the people hardy; used to survival at the multi-cultural crossroads of Eastern Russia, Central Asia and Mongolia that was Irkutsk, a city of 600,000 or so. This was where the dissenting Russian nobility, the Decembrists, were sent in the early 1800s and where summers were only two months long. The structure of the Soviet Union was gone, but nothing had really taken its place: there was uncertainty and poverty, opportunism and unfettered capitalism. There were abundant new products for the first time in decades. Some of the alcoholic street wanderers were known as *pedigrichiki* since they had found that the new imported dog food was cheap, nourishing and pretty digestible with a bottle of beer.

The most wonderful period of our time in Siberia was spent in a village called Lower Katchergat, discovered through an artist, called Lena and her husband, Kolya. I had called into a small exhibition of artists and fallen into conversation with Lena and bought a couple of her watercolours. She had invited us to visit her dacha for the weekend in Katchergat, about 100km east of Irkutsk, just north of the Baikal coastline. I had only met her for 10 minutes but had decided to accept the invitation and with no map, mobile phone or GPS – just directions – we set off in the trusty *Niva* (small Lada 4x4) on a Friday afternoon. Just Zoe, me and Muffin.

It was dark by the time we had travelled along 90km of forest track, through ever thinning villages and over ever-increasing potholes, but we bounced along, brimming with innocent hope and a fairly-full fuel tank. I knew we must be nearing our destination from the distance travelled and then in the murky evening light, under a forest covered canopy, I spotted across the road a lowered red and white striped metal barrier and a man, standing, watching us. Over his shoulder, a rifle. I felt a slight movement of my lower stomach. I suddenly remembered my touring days in East Germany, when the Tour Navigator, always a Sergeant Major figure, would occasionally say, as we were making our final approach to the intelligence target: 'Boss, the only way out is the way in,' at which point, you gripped yourself for the possibility that you may become boxed in or need to do a very fast reverse followed by a handbrake turn. I may indeed have muttered the same to Zoe and Muffin at this point, but in any case we drove edgily towards the armed figure in the least aggressive way possible, hoping he would not open fire before we could offer a dry-throated English-sounding question: 'I say, is this Lower Katchergat?' Good news – the rifle remained on the shoulder, new faces and different worlds met, greetings were exchanged, directions given. The reason for the guard was that there had been recent thefts of horses from the area – perhaps a roving band of Siberian cowboys engaged in rustling. Thankfully, that night the only rustling was the sound of the Siberian winter wind whipping the top of the pine forest while we were tucked up in a warm wooden log cabin, on the start of another adventure.

A number of historic events took place in Irkutsk as the country emerged from the stranglehold of the Soviet legacy. The Catholic Church was opened for the first time since the revolution, by a wonderful man called Father Ignatius, who was a Polish priest and an orphan of the Second World War.

I took Zoe on a drive round the city and she spotted a 'hopeful drinker', standing on the side of the road as if thumbing a lift, but actually extending the thumb and little finger up and down respectively with the middle three fingers folded across the palm like a symbol of a telephone receiver. Zoe said: 'Stop, he wants to make a phone call.' I countered: 'No, Zoe, he wants to buy vodka and will do almost anything to get it.' We drove on.

In wanting to live healthily, we befriended the director of the Irkutsk meat market, Viktor, a positive-thinking former army major and still a devout Communist. We often drank 'Soviet champagne' in his office and afterwards he would allow me to walk with him into his huge frozen meat store and choose some relatively fresh cuts of beef. He confided that several of the carcasses there were over ten years old.

There were no supermarkets in Irkutsk in 1992 so a trip to the supermarket meant that Zoe, Muffin and I had to board an SU-130 for a seven-hour flight to Moscow, with Muffin allowed to walk freely round the cabin and be fed by friendly Siberians. Once in Moscow, we stayed the night in the company apartment on Tverskaia and went to Stockmanns, the Swedish supermarket, which had what were then simply marvellous treasures, goods that would adorn any supermarket shelf now. The only place we wanted to eat was a Pizza Hut or Pizza Land on Tverskaia, where for an hour we could step out of the Soviet system that engulfed us in body and mind.

My American boss, Larry, had a theory about the Aeroflot chicken portions that were served on every SU-130 flight. They were scrawny, grey-blue pieces of meat and Larry was convinced that Aeroflot had a long-term agreement with some 'Chicken Kombinat' to buy only chickens that had died of old age.

One day I was sitting on an SU-130 waiting for it to taxi from its icy Irkutsk stand on a slight slope and as soon as we started to taxi the aircraft alarmingly slid several metres to the left, getting close to the terminal. Another time, I waited for ages as the engines wound up and down, each failing to start on the first attempt. Some years after we left, I saw the report of an awful crash that had led to the loss of all lives on the same SU-130 Irkutsk-Moscow flight, due to multiple engine failure.

I was eventually fired from my post as Deputy Manager, Brooke-Taiga Timber Joint Venture, for upsetting the local management by reporting to my US bosses that they had signed a sales agreement with two entities for the same pile of timber at Nakhodkat. At least I was taken out for a farewell dinner. I learned later that my successor, another Brit joining from TNT in Moscow, had not been so lucky and had apparently had a gun held to his head and been given 24 hours to leave Irkutsk. That made my sacking seem palatable.

One of the things I had difficulty in explaining to my New York BTT-JV boss was that there were two days, which were not holidays, when the sawmill factory would absolutely have to close. Day One was selected according to the weather in June when the potatoes had to be planted and the entire town made a mass exodus to dachas and fields around the city, boarding buses with their spades, the ends wrapped in cloth. Day Two was a day in August, when, again the whole JV went out to bring the potatoes in – vital in order to keep families fed during the harsh winter temperatures of minus 18 to 25C.

Zoe had help at home with the washing and ironing from Vika, a young girl, who was highly recommended by someone we should not have listened to. We admit that the iron was not the latest auto steam version, but it did not explain why Vika in order to dampen the shirt took a mouthful of water from a cup and spat it out onto the board. Vika did not last very long.

Zoe put up with more than I now realise was ever fair. She was mostly alone all day with no friends, apart from Muffin, speaking not a word of Russian while living in a remote Siberian city. The only way to ring home was to order a call via Novosibirsk operators, who did not tolerate stuttering pidgin Russian and often slammed down the receiver. I came home one day to find our Panasonic cordless in several pieces and scattered around the room.

I also knew that the kitchen tap had been dripping increasingly. Zoe called me at 9.30 one morning, to say that the hot water tap in the kitchen had blown, was gushing and the flat was full of steam. I asked for help and rushed home to wait for the plumber. It seemed like forever, but eventually Lena the neighbour came in and said that the plumber was waiting downstairs. 'Downstairs?' I fumed. 'Why downstairs?' 'He only has one leg, you have to carry him up,' came the reply.

Zoe made one good friend, who could speak English and who gave herself an English name, Nancy. Nancy became pregnant and was advised to stop taking baths, in case she caught an infection from the water. There was nothing much wrong with the water, but that was Soviet medicine for you.

Health is a free-for-all subject in the former Soviet Union. Should you make the 'mistake' of allowing your child to walk down the street on a cool morning, you were likely to be assailed by one *babushka* after another, demanding accusingly: '*Pochemu bez shapki?*' (Why no hat?)

The saddest thing I ever saw was on the staircase a level below our fourth floor apartment. I came out to walk Muffin one winter day and on the staircase, kneeling in her coat, was an old woman, who had a block of wood and on it a raw white oxtail. She wobbled a small crude axe and sobbed as she tried to hack off tiny slivers from the bony tail. I was deeply shocked that this was one of my neighbours and went back up to our floor. On our landing they told me that this woman had been a state prosecutor in Soviet times and since the collapse of the Soviet Union had lost her privileges and no-one had any time for her. She had locked up many a person, possibly unfairly. I could not bear it and took her round a hamper of food; she never spoke, but just cried as I passed it to her.

When I finally left Irkutsk after eighteen months of baptism by Siberian fire, I remember two events. One was getting our 36 boxes of possessions from the apartment to Moscow TNT at Domodedovo airport in the early summer of 1993. This is how it went: I was alone, as Zoe had left earlier for Moscow with Muffin; the boxes were packed in our fourth floor apartment. I went outside and hired two guys from the street to carry the boxes down with me. I piled them on the street and then stopped a truck and hired him to take me to the airport. Everyone was grateful for the dollars and I was generous because I had a plane to catch, the good old SU-130 Irkutsk to Moscow. My truck delivered me to the cargo area for Aeroflot and the next thing I remember was driving up to the plane and physically loading the boxes myself into the hold. I drove back round to the main terminal building, checked in and flew on the same plane to 'Domy'.

There were also two surreal experiences at Domodedovo, one of Moscow's main internal airports. I was again at the cargo area, waiting for my boxes to arrive from the flight in order to hand them over to TNT. While I was waiting, I observed the activity at the freight yard. There was a bustling movement of forklifts on the summer evening and I saw one forklift precariously loaded with crates of dark grapes. The driver suddenly stopped his forklift in the middle of the yard and shouted loudly *'rebiata!'* (guys!). Immediately, everyone stopped and dropped whatever they were doing and descended on the forklift and simply plundered the load, stuffing bunches of grapes into their mouths, pockets and bags. This lasted for about two minutes and the forklift then carried on and everyone went back to their tasks. While all this was happening, I had noticed a solitary simple wooden coffin, with no paperwork and just a single red rose lying on it. Eventually, my boxes arrived and so did TNT and I remember the total relief of falling into the safe arms of the modern world of commercial logistics.

The other unforgettable moment was a 'lesson of life' in the Soviet Union that I took with me for years to come. Muffin, as you know, was used to travelling on SU-130 as a freeloader, looking for scraps up and down the aisle, but I knew that from Moscow Sheremetevo to Paris we would need to check the rules on carriage of pets. I had called Moscow Aeroflot from Irkutsk and was told that if the animal was less than 15kg, she could travel in the cabin with us on our lap. Phew! Muffin went on a crash diet and to emphasise her trim figure when we checked in, I carried her in a rucksack on my back. We went through immigration, checked in, received boarding cards, but when we went to the departure lounge a girl said: 'You can't take that dog on board. It must be in a crate'. Zoe loved Muffin more deeply and passionately than anyone. Yes, anyone. I felt not only the sweaty heat of a Cocker Spaniel pressing on my back, I also felt that deep sicky feeling of knowing that something critical to a relationship was about to go horribly wrong. 'What can we do?' *'Nel'zia'* (Not allowed). 'Who can we talk to?' This fraught conversation dragged on, I becoming ever more desperate as I watched Zoe's tense face. Eventually, we were referred to the supervisor, who also refused permission, but finally said: 'You will need to talk with the head of the shift.' 'OK, where is he?' 'His office is back in the main hall of the airport'. So back I went through all the previous check points, poor Muffin still in the slow-cooker rucksack, and reached the main hall only to find the office closed and empty. I had a moment of sheer panic and nausea, followed instantly by the best idea I ever had. I visualised that he was sitting there in his office and that I asked my question and that he smiled at me kindly and said *'konechno'* (of course). Emboldened by my virtual answer, I strode back through officialdom and announced confidently to the girls that he had said it was fine. They did not blink, question or hesitate, but just nodded and waved us through.

What I did at that moment in the main hall of Sheremetevo in 1993, was to grasp one of the fundamental rules of survival in the post-Soviet era, which, I think, still applies today. If you remove the fear and burden of responsibility for making decisions from people, you release them and unblock situations that appear illogical and unsolvable. So always start at the top of the chain and work down, not the other way round. By the way, Muffin behaved like a lady on the flight to Paris and my conscience was – and is – clean, and so was the Aeroflot carpet.

Ukraine, the passing of Muffin, too much vodka

We moved to Kiev in 1993, where I had been sent with Zoe and Muffin with Thomas De La Rue, the British banknote printers, to be the local manager responsible for setting up Ukraine's first banknote factory. I was less surprised to be in Kiev than I thought, as the whole affair had been predicted by medium Madame Ghosh and told to Zoe while she waited for her friend to have a medium's reading in a hotel at Russell Square in London. My UK colleagues at De La Rue were impressed that I was heading to the wilds of Eastern Europe until I explained to them that Kiev was a doddle compared with the wilds of Siberia and that living only three hours from Blighty was sheer luxury. When we arrived in October 1993, Ukraine was mired in hyper-inflation, and there were only two places in Kiev that accepted credit cards – a restaurant and a supermarket. The expat pioneers who had witnessed the Soviet Union break-up were leaving after their third year, with stories that made mine sound lame. I remember walking down Kreshchatik, the main street in central Kiev, and thinking that there was still dullness in many people's eyes. Looking back, it was probably more a weariness; it was a tremendously challenging and harsh time for the older generation. Their hard-earned rouble pensions had evaporated. Anyone paid in hard currency was, by definition, wealthy and if you could get a job with a foreign company or Embassy, you were a very lucky Ukrainian.

It was in Kiev that we lost Muffin. I inadvertently left a rubbish bag accessible to her and she had rummaged through it and found chicken bones, resulting in painful peritonitis and the urgent need for an operation. We knew no vets and there were only Soviet-style clinics that Zoe could not bear to visit. Our driver, Sasha took us to meet his friend and private vet, called Anatoly, who normally operated in the kitchen of his two-roomed apartment. He took one look at Muffin and said he could save her, but he needed to operate now. We refused and flew her to Frankfurt, where it was too late and she died. They say a loss can create opportunity and as a result of what happened to Muffin, Zoe decided to help Anatoly to open what we think was the first private veterinary clinic in Kiev and possibly in Ukraine. The clinic still operates today.

In Kiev we made true friendships with Ukrainians and learned the nuances of being entertained in homes, with all the traditions of eating and drinking. If it is true that the type of alcohol a nation drinks reflects their quality of life, then vodka reinforces that. It is a harsh drink, often drunk to excess and with significant results, both short and long term, that are not all negative.

The truth is that you can strike a deep and strong human relationship with someone in one night over vodka, much more so than during a year of our English middle-class 'you must come over and see us sometime' dinner parties, where the positioning of the cutlery and the delicacy of conversation can take priority over conversation and friendship. No, the Slav version is straightforward. Enter the home, be greeted by hugs and kisses, go straight to and sit at the table and do not leave it all night except to adjust oneself. From the start of the evening the table is covered with plates of cold food, salads, fresh vegetables, cold fish and meat dishes and bottles of soft and hard drink in the centre. None of our 'have a gin and tonic' in the sitting room and then 'do come into the dining room'. When all are seated around the table, the host will propose the first toast to our meeting and the head guest replies with the next toast. The third Ukrainian toast is traditionally to the ladies and is drunk standing. As much as you may try, you cannot physiologically protect yourself from the effects of vodka toasts. Sure, you can drink milk beforehand and eat your fill from the first cold salad course to line the stomach. Yes, you can risk regurgitating the vodka back into your mineral water or juice, but, if the host notices, you had best forget any chance of mutual trust being established. It is a raw, human exchange of energy, humour, good wishes and statements from the heart. Like most Western men, I never choose to drink vodka on its own or on my own, but when in the company of good friends, the drinking of sincere toasts binds you as close as when you collectively survive a scary venture and the result is simple – trust. That trust, if it is established over a business dinner, will mean that the contract that is signed the next day is founded on genuinely-expressed statements the night before. It begs the question; what happens when we are affected deeply by alcohol – do we reveal our true selves or do we act out a role? From my experience, the former is true.

Never make the classic, first-time, Western-guests-in-a-Ukrainian-home mistake where you walk in, see the cold platter dishes covering the entire table, dig in deep and then lean back, patting the tummy, exclaiming, 'Ah, that was truly fantastic.' For there will follow the slow relentless torture of the soup course, which is a meal in itself, and after that there will be the main hot course, heavy with thick meat, gravy and potatoes. That is followed by cake, fruit, ice cream and chocolates. You cannot leave the table except to seek temporary relief in the bathroom, where the window is now too small to climb through. In fact, there is no bathroom window since you are on the twelfth floor of an apartment block. You will be truly exhausted and suffering and will never make the same mistake again – unless the vodka gets the better of you.

The Turkmen, Kazakhs, Uzbeks and Kyrgyz, whom I also know well, are no less generous. The Turkmen have a saying: '*Gost' vyshe otsa*', or 'the guest is higher than the father', meaning when you enter a Turkmen home you are accorded more respect (and vodka) than the father of the household.

I end this short tale with a reflection. The beauty of a foreign language is that it gives you an opportunity to dive deeply and quickly into a totally different life experience. The only other attributes you need are openness and the willingness to exchange energy with someone, to listen, to learn and to give something of your life experiences. I have one or two customers who are now friends for life, with whom I maintain close contact. As one grows older and possibly wiser, you realise that these kinds of relationships provide the type of foundation that makes you truly happy.

There is much in the politics of the whole former Soviet region that is discouraging and negative and it may well be a long time before there are leaders that truly care about what happens to ordinary people. But there are, and I think there always will be, as anywhere, great individuals who have something valuable, precious and fun to offer. You might occasionally feel like coming up for air and occasionally may need to go West and readjust at home, but the likelihood is that you will want to go back. I say, if you learn Russian, you are lucky. If you possibly can, take what you have learned and go out there and enjoy the experience and make it a life-long adventure.

Will Stamper studied Slavonic Studies (Russian and Serbo-Croat) at the University of Nottingham from 1979 to 1983. He was sponsored through university by the British Army and in 1983 joined his local infantry battalion, 1 STAFFORDS. He served in Northern Ireland, West Germany and the Gulf War. His next Russian experience was serving in Berlin with BRIXMIS (The British Commanders'-in-Chief Mission to the Soviet Forces in Germany), where he caught the last six months of BRIXMIS operations as a tour officer, working in East Germany, before the re-unification of Germany in 1990. After leaving the Army in 1991, he moved to Irkutsk, Siberia, in his first civilian job as a manager in a US-Russian timber joint venture. In 1993 he then joined De La Rue, the British bank note printers and continued living in Kiev with his family until 2008.

All the world's a stage

Learning Russian transported **Rachel Farmer** *into a land of 'make-believe' where she befriends her literary heroes and sells dog-flaps to a sceptical Russian public*

Vladimir Nikolaevich Voinovich is a Russian writer and former dissident, whose works were banned in the Brezhnev period. His telephone was cut off in 1976 and his family was forced to emigrate in 1980. He became popular in the West and his citizenship was restored by Mikhail Gorbachev in 1990. Voinovich won many international awards and honour titles, including the State Prize of the Russian Federation (2000) and the Andrei Sakharov Prize for Writers' Civic Courage (2002).

FROM my first introduction to the Russian language and culture as a schoolgirl in the 1960s in Nottingham, I have been fascinated by the theatrical quality of Russian history and culture. You simply could not make it up if you tried and it was a while before I truly believed in the existence of Russia at all.

Russian language and literature at school tantalised but did not persuade me, and it was not until my Russian teacher, Alan Richards, gathered the class under the bonnet of his new Moskvich car that I became a believer. There, in real Cyrillic letters formed for real Russian eyes, were instructions on what to do to the engine when the temperature fell below minus twenty degrees. The kopeck dropped and the improbably cosy tales of Haywood's *A First Russian Book* gave way to reality.

Russia, or rather the Soviet Union when I first visited as a student from the University of Birmingham in the mid-1970s, was exciting and unpredictable. It was a place where things happened that could not be explained; where there was a sensation of being on stage and of being the only person who had not seen the script. Rules were apparently made to be broken and the professed rejection of Western values was given the lie by the constant furtive clamour for Western jeans, tights, paperbacks and chewing gum.

The contrast of tiny jewel-like churches set in a grey sea of concrete housing blocks, the scale and sweep of the landscape and the climate, the emotional energy of the people, with their noise and deep silences, their explosive anger and their warmth, their sentimentality and subtlety – all of these appealed enormously to the girl from a quiet orderly family of schoolteachers, where emotions were kept safely at the shallow end of the paddling pool.

I began my studies as a joint Russian and French student, but ditched the French for what I perceived as the far more interesting and exotic Serbo-Croat and Old Church Slavonic combo. The downside of this was that my degree course stipulated that I should spend just seven weeks in a Russian-speaking environment, rather than the full year accorded to students of more mainstream languages.

Four weeks in Moscow provided a welcome reality check and a glorious first impression of Russian life, although we were all so paranoid about being bugged and followed that we clustered together in a linguistically unproductive way. Having had little exposure to real live Russians at university, we were surprised to find that, although we could read Tolstoi and Dostoevsky with relative ease, we had no idea how to speak Russian and did not know the words for many everyday objects. Intonation was an unknown dark art, and we would boldly tell people to get off the bus, believing that we were asking them politely whether they were about to alight!

We were issued with a group of 'official friends', who attempted to escort us everywhere and it became something of a game to try to give them the slip. I remember slipping away for long enough to visit a Protestant church in the woods on the edge of the city, simply out of curiosity. At the church I was instantly issued with another 'official friend' to prevent me from talking to anyone more 'real'. He rather attached himself to me, turning up at the hostel, presenting me with a boxed set of *Lebedinoe ozero* (Swan Lake) on 'Melodiia' vinyl, and suggesting various improper and un-Protestant activities. I had to give him the slip too.

Slipping away was not easy in those days. We were easily distinguishable by our clothing and by the fact that the females had shaven legs and the males unshaven faces. We were betrayed too by our tendency to smile too readily and to display affection towards each other, which behaviour drew reprimands and cries of 'hippy' and 'hooligan'.

The journey to Moscow on this first visit was by train across Europe, which included the unforgettable experience of being locked in the carriages at the Polish-Russian border while the train was lifted up and the wheels changed to accommodate the different gauge – all under the watchful eye of armed Polish guards.

On the return journey, a friend and I jumped train in Amsterdam, so bedazzled were we by the bright lights, the colourful billboards and the temptations of the West after a month of mostly grey.

A British Council-sponsored trip to Leningrad in the early spring of my final year at university exposed me to the beauties of that city and taught me that cold weather provided better cover for running around incognito, since coat and hat would meet somewhere mid-face. Of course, taking my hat off because I was too hot would bring a hail of rebukes from wise old ladies who knew better.

Life moved on. I completed my degree, married, took a Post-Graduate Certificate of Education at the University of Nottingham and became a schoolteacher of Russian and French. In the late 1970s, parents of pupils opting for Russian were openly suspicious of my politics and motivations and would have preferred their children to choose German or Spanish. Some would tell me they didn't want their children to be influenced by someone who must have Communist sympathies and, anyway, what possible use could Russian ever be? Over the years I developed a portfolio of Russian classes all over the East Midlands, working in schools, colleges, a prison and with private and corporate individual students. The prison work arose in the enlightened and well-funded years of prison education when, if an offender expressed an interest in a subject, a teacher was found for him or her if at all possible. I worked in a prison for 'vulnerable' offenders, in other words sex offenders, policemen, judges and spies, who would have had a rough ride in an ordinary prison. This particular prison housed offenders who were close to release and their educational opportunities were many and various. Because of the nature of their offences, care had to be taken in checking that their motivation was pure. For example, some would seek to study catering in order to find employment in a school kitchen and some would seek to learn a particular language because of that country's low age of sexual consent. Russian was judged to be a genuine interest for several men, so I was brought in to teach them. At one point, I was teaching Russian to a man in prison while at the same time teaching it to his daughter in school.

I was once given permission to take a male Russian visitor into the prison to speak Russian to my group and to answer their questions. Leonid, who had survived the siege of Leningrad as a child and had experienced many hardships in life, was astounded and rather outraged at the lives of the offenders, which included not only Russian lessons but also three square meals a day, paid work, TV, cigarettes, gardening, a library, football and a mini golf course. 'This is not a prison; this is a health resort!' he exclaimed as he arm-wrestled a rapist. 'What do I have to do to get locked up in here?'

In short, I spread the good news of Russian language and culture wherever people would listen. My career was neither planned nor co-ordinated and there were gaps for having children and times when because of circumstances I taught only French and lost track of Russian completely.

After one such gap I went on a Soviet-sponsored refresher course for teachers of Russian, which consisted of a month's intensive language classes at the Herzen Institute in Leningrad. This was a real stimulus to learning and, upon my return I approached the Department of Slavonic Studies at the University of Nottingham with a view to doing an MPhil in some area of Soviet literature.

I settled upon the life and works of Vladimir Voinovich, author of *The Life and Extraordinary Adventures of Private Ivan Chonkin*, largely because his writing made me laugh, even though 'through tears'. I thought that close proximity to some of the more tragic Soviet literature, particularly the poetry, would have had me in despair by breakfast every day and, while emotions of despair were undoubtedly part of the charm of Russian literature, I thought that this might become trying over a long period. Hence Voinovich.

The life and works of Voinovich turned out to be highly engaging and I thoroughly enjoyed converting an MPhil into a PhD, rising at 4am to fit my research into a timetable that was busy by this time with teaching language to beginners in the Department of Slavonic Studies and evening classes elsewhere. The balance of working with bright young students and spending solitary hours alone with my computer and a pile of books was perfect.

I visited libraries in Moscow and St Petersburg on many occasions, becoming only slightly irritated by the necessity to fill in countless forms in order to get sight of texts and then to repeat the process and wait several days to get photocopies of them. The glamour of sitting in dusty, dimly-lit reading rooms watching the snow fall outside and hunting through card indexes was reward in itself. My quest for research material was greatly aided by Martin Dewhirst of the University of Glasgow who sent me regular envelopes stuffed with relevant cuttings about Voinovich, who I by now referred to as VV.

So imagine my excitement – and horror – when my supervisor, Lesley Milne, told me that VV was coming to the UK and that it would be highly desirable for me to interview him. How

I wished at that moment that I had studied a dead writer. I briefly considered assassinating him. I wondered what he would make of the presumption of a random British woman having written thousands of words about him without ever having met him. What if he was grumpy or incomprehensible or uncommunicative or disagreed with everything I had written? In the event, he was delightful, charmed by my interest and exceedingly talkative. A lifelong friendship was formed.

At the same time as teaching and researching, I had taken the opportunity to study Serbian for a couple of years in the Slavonic Studies department at Nottingham alongside a small group of students. I have always found it beneficial as a language teacher to do occasional night classes in unknown languages to remind me of what it is like to sit on the other side of the desk and to empathise with those students who tremble as their 'turn' to speak approaches.

This was the perfect opportunity. Although I had studied Serbo-Croat as part of my first degree it was not the sort of study that led to being able to say anything, so I was delighted and daunted in equal measure to join Dr Vladislava Ribnikar's class of awesomely clever students. My credibility was at stake here so I threw myself into study with great energy.

At the end of two years studying Serbian and at the same time as completing my PhD – which felt simultaneously like a bereavement and a happy release – I was told by the Serbian/Croatian section of the Department that I was eligible to go to Belgrade for a month on a language and culture course sponsored by the Serbian government for students of Serbian from around the world. Occasionally I have been asked to recall my favourite holiday and this trip to Belgrade (although not meant to be a holiday) always springs to mind. The combination of daily language classes, cultural events, singing, dancing and endless walking around the city and browsing in bookshops was my idea of heaven.

After three weeks in the city even I became slightly tired of the people, the dust and heat and was relieved when we were taken by bus, via a folk dancing festival, to Kopaonik, a ski resort high in the mountains. As it was summer, there were few people there but for the first few days there was thick and persistent fog. My frustration at being confined to the hotel and language classes with teachers who were by now flagging, was hard to conceal. On the morning of the third day I awoke early to bright sunshine and a view of mountain peaks and, without leaving a message and without a thought about health and safety, I crept out and made a beeline up the route of the ski lift to the first summit. From there, I could see the way that the mountains were grouped around the resort and how it should be possible to walk from one to another in a huge loop, providing the fog did not return. Then began one of the finest days of my life. Like something out of *The Sound of Music*, I cavorted across meadows and clambered up and down slopes with nothing but a bottle of water and a few blueberries to sustain me. The sky remained blue, not even I could get lost with everything spread out before me like a map, and I met only one solitary goat-herd.

After completing my PhD, I was seized by the desire to spend more time in Russia than I had done previously and to devote some time to improving my language skills. A permanent move to Russia was out of the question because of teenage children at home, but I managed to arrange matters domestically in a way which made six months' absence just about feasible.

I enrolled on a European-funded programme where graduates were hired by UK companies to carry out research or promote their business in an overseas market. The UK businesses got access to cheap brains and the cheap brains got access to an adventure overseas and enough money to live on for six months. I was chosen by a Grimsby fish smoker and merchant, whose speciality was 'smoked dog flaps'. These are the belly flaps of the dog fish which, when smoked, curl into ringlet shapes. My fish merchant was a bit of a dashing entrepreneurial figure in Grimsby, driving something fast and glamorous and boasting an interesting private life.

For several months I drove back and forth to Grimsby in my ancient VW Beetle to learn about the business before being dispatched to Moscow to share a flat with another set of cheap brains in the form of a lovely young woman, Natasha, whose mission was to sell tanning beds to the Russian market. Like me, she was seeking an opportunity to try out her Russian for real. While she was touting tanning beds, my task was to find sources of raw unprocessed fish which could be imported to Grimsby, and to research the Russian taste in smoked fish to see whether 'smoked dog flaps' or other delicacies could be exported for the Russian table.

I enlisted VV in the search for suitable accommodation and he sent an address and promised to be there when we arrived. Our arrival was early in January 1998 in a howling blizzard and Natasha and I climbed the stairs to the eighth floor in the dark because of a power cut which meant that the lift was not working.

VV opened the door and showed us into a tiny shabby flat with walls covered in wallpaper from 1939 and a range of bizarre and disturbing paintings. He introduced us to our landlord, the artist Nikolai Postnikov, who was responsible for the artwork. Postnikov's mother had died recently in the flat, which explained its availability and also explained the memorabilia stuffed in all the cupboards and drawers, including her false teeth. Her spirit seemed still to live on in the flat and on International Women's Day I awoke to answer the phone to a long and prepared speech from an old lady wishing me happiness, health, success and the rest, which was clearly intended for the late Mrs P. I had to break it to her that her friend was no longer with us.

When we arrived at the flat, another person also greeted us, sitting on an upright chair with queenly dignity as if granting us an audience. I guessed she must be someone of note, but she introduced herself simply as Lucy and I was at a loss to place her until I realised after a few minutes that she must be Liudmila Petrushevskaia, a complete eccentric and absolutely my favourite contemporary writer – apart from Voinovich. She lived just up the road and made me very welcome during our stay, taking me to the local market, to the nearby Sokol'niki Park and to jazz clubs, and reading to me from work in progress. I could have been tempted to start on another PhD but probably one is enough in a lifetime unless one starts a great deal earlier than I did.

The end of the 1990s was a lawless time and on the first Friday night of our stay a young policeman was shot dead outside our house. That was not the only fatal drama on our street. However, it was a time of transition and stability was gradually being established, albeit unlawfully.

During this time I was happily engaged in a whirl of literary soirees and cultural privilege, bestowed on me by the kindness of VV. Perhaps the crowning glory of these cultural events was an occasion when I met up with him in St Petersburg and went as his guest to the tenth-anniversary celebrations of the Russian Museum, which were held in the splendour of the Catherine Palace. Everyone around the vast candlelit table was a cultural figure or a director of a prestigious museum, except for me. I rather enjoyed introducing myself as an Englishwoman working for a Grimsby fish merchant.

In terms of my fishy mission, I did a lot of market research and ate many kilos of fish, smoked and otherwise. Fortunately fish is one of my favourite foods. I joined a fishy Scottish trade mission and visited many fish processing plants. I beat a path to the doors of merchants and distributors and set up meetings for my boss when he visited, which he did several times, each time bearing several stone of frozen smoked fish samples in his hand luggage. The samples were liberally distributed to all my fishy contacts and many friends, who declared them to be very good, but by the end of my stay I had built up such a backlog that I had to give the last few packs to the local cats as everyone else had eaten their fill.

Whenever the fish merchant came to town I would look forward to being briefly transported from my relatively squalid existence in the flat to a life of luxury. In the flat Natasha and I waged war on the cockroaches with a heavy frying pan and 'the lad' from next door slept on our landing. The wastrel 'lad' was forty if he was a day, had a serious alcohol problem and had been thrown out of his own flat by his father, who had rented out his son's room to a stranger. Occasionally his mother would let 'the lad' in and feed him but most of the time he slept in the basement or across our doormat. The advent of the Grimsby fish merchant meant being whisked away for a few hours to posh restaurants and a cultural programme which I was at liberty to arrange at his expense.

I flew with him to Murmansk, which was both enlightening and also very light as it was nearly the time of white nights. Despite being the home of several trawler fleets, there was hardly a fish to be seen in Murmansk as all catches were routinely diverted under the counter to Norway. The ships would then return to port and complain of disastrous bad luck at sea, whilst pocketing the cash. Strangely, there was plenty of naïve EU money going into developing fish processing plants in Murmansk, although these plants were distinguished more by their luxurious saunas and lodges than by the presence of a single fish.

The fish merchant was rather bemused by the challenges of Russia but he was a truly adventurous spirit and he had the sort of stamina required to cope with features such as enforced alcoholic socialising, businesses bristling with heavily-armed guards, and restaurants which locked you inside while you ate your caviar and quaffed 'Soviet champagne'.

Back in Moscow, business was developing more hopefully and the fish merchant was getting excited about the possibility of success and of cocking a snook at his competition back home who had not had the foresight to employ a Russian-speaking brain. But when the devaluation and default crisis of 1998 hit, his potential business partners went bust and everything fell apart.

At least the fish merchant and I could return to the UK relatively unscathed, but it was a different story for my friends in Moscow and for thousands like them who had for a brief while felt as if they were climbing out of the hard times into an emerging middle class. They suddenly had the rug pulled from under them. Yet again.

The fishy episode served as my introduction to business, both UK-style and Russian-style, and set me on a course away from academia and towards enterprise. I returned briefly to teaching Russian at the University of Nottingham, but soon moved on to a business environment which was faster-moving, less stable and more 'edgy' – which is probably the word I would choose to sum up the attractions of Russia for me.

For some years I managed a range of UK training organisations with no connection at all to Russian, but I always kept the Russian theme in the background through occasional visits, bits of freelance work delivering cultural and language training, contact with friends and piles of books.

When I set up my own training business in 2006, it was with a view to bringing together my two favourite themes of training and Russia, but it took a few years of positioning myself and reviving my rusty language skills before I was ready to dive in. I was fortunate in getting a toehold in the Moscow market at my first attempt, being commissioned by a major international oil and gas company to deliver cultural training to their expat managers and spouses in the kitsch buildings of the Izmailovsky kremlin. It was only a day, but it set me on my way.

The sense that I am still on stage without a script has not left me, even though the environment has become more stable, more westernised and more familiar to me. Much of this narrative has been written whilst working in Kazakhstan or Russia, experiencing that mixture of exhilaration and exhaustion which comes from extremes of temperature, language overload and a turbo-charged diet.

Age and nascent wisdom bring me a previously absent awareness of risk. Working largely in the oil and gas industry with all its potential hazards and having been uncomfortably close to a suicide bomber in Kazakhstan have made me wonder briefly about my choice of work, even though the unfortunate man's detonation was alleged to be premature and accidental and his proximity to me must therefore have been purely coincidental. Still, there is such a thing as fate in the Russian mindset and I can sometimes be seen spitting thrice over the left shoulder – 'tfoo, tfoo, tfoo' – to take care.

As well as an awareness of risk, age has also brought me into contact with a different demographic group in Russia. Although I am far from retirement age in the UK, my female contemporaries in Russia are already starting to draw their pensions and slow down their working lives. I remember older colleagues at the University of Nottingham telling me when I was in my thirties that I would no longer want to go to Russia once I got to fifty as it was just too exhausting. They had a point but perhaps Russia is not quite as gruelling as it once was. In any case, I am still enjoying it even though I am well past their benchmark.

On a recent visit to Krasnodar, I was enjoying an early evening jog through the park past the open-air dance floor where the pensioners were gyrating in their coats and hats to piped music. They stared at me for being improperly dressed in the cold, but did not call out as they might have done in Soviet times. As I was running towards the park exit an elderly lady in a pea-green coat with a beautiful gold-plated smile stepped in front of me and accosted me with 'Where are you going? Come and join the dance!' and, seizing me by both hands, whisked me over to the merry throng. Being in jogging mode I was happy to dance my socks off with her, but drew the line at the man with Cossack whiskers and rows of steel teeth who wanted to twirl me around and take me for a spin in his motor.

While loving the spontaneity of living on stage in Russia, I find these days that you don't always have to read the script to make wise decisions.

Rachel Farmer studied at the University of Birmingham, then took a PGCE at the University of Nottingham. Her working life has revolved around teaching and training, in schools, colleges, prisons and at the university. She was awarded her PhD while also studying Serbian and authoring Russian courses. She set up a training business, delivering language training in Russia, Kazakhstan and the UK. Her work focuses mainly on international management, and assessment and verification skills.

Crime, punishment and investigative psychology

***Marion Bates** exported UK criminal profiling techniques to Moscow and succeeded in winning over hardened homicide detectives*

The forerunner of the Moscow City Police was established in 1722, shortly after Peter the Great had in St Petersburg created the first Russian police force. It is currently the largest municipal police force in the Russian Federation with primary responsibility for law enforcement and investigation within Moscow.

NUMBER 38, Ulitsa Petrovka strikes fear into the heart of most Muscovites, indeed most Russians. It is the headquarters of the Moscow City Police, the Russian Scotland Yard. It sits somewhat incongruously in the Tverskoi district amid the smart hotels, bars and boutiques which have spread out from the centre and is just a few streets away from one of the smartest shopping areas of the new Moscow. I often wonder how I found myself in the boiling hot July of 2002 advising this feared and secretive force on the use of geographical profiling techniques.

As an adolescent growing up in a leafy suburb of Kent, I went on the standard week-long school trip, which included an overnight romantic train trip between Moscow and Leningrad complete with boiling hot tea in glasses, fierce *provodnitsa*[4] and

---

[4] Carriage attendant/conductress

dawn views of fishermen on glistening lakes. All this was set against the grimness of our large tower block hotel near Yugo-Zapadnaia, kick-starting my obsession with the paradoxical nature of Russia (and the former Soviet Union). A place of extremes, the darker side of Russian and Soviet culture captivated me and I began private Russian lessons in my A-level years and ended up applying to study Russian.

My teenage view that Communism was a sound idea began to be challenged the more I discovered about what lay behind the cardboard cut-out baddies of Stalinism, the Gulags, the Lubianka and the immense power of the State. At the same time, the more I read, the more I wondered in awe at the beauty of the literature and architecture that continued to survive in the face of unendurable hardship. I fell in love with the study of Soviet poetry, literature and theatre. I adored the poetry of Akhmatova, Tsvetaeva and became obsessed with Chekhov and Gorky. Even being followed in our first year summer trip to Russia in 1990, by a diligent young student whom we thought, rightly or wrongly, a KGB informer, seemed romantic to me.

A year living as a student in Kiev and Moscow in 1991-2 really opened my eyes to the privations suffered by the people of the Soviet Union. We were privileged to witness the first trickle of change from Communism to democracy and yet we were still able to travel from Moscow to Kamchatka for next to nothing on our student tickets – post-Soviet freedom at Soviet prices. Hindsight is a wonderful thing of course and perhaps my glasses have a rosy tint now, but I haven't forgotten how hard it was living in Kiev during a food shortage and going to sleep in our hostel in coats and *shapki*[5] because a fuel dispute with Moscow meant our central heating was cut off. Our teachers would bring us breakfast and we would eat suppers of kebabs in the Azerbaijani kebab house nearby. I soon gave up my vegetarianism.

In my final year at Nottingham, I was to read Dostoevsky's *Crime and Punishment*. Before or since, I have never been

---

[5] Russian fur hats

so profoundly affected by any book, fiction or non-fiction. To my twenty-year-old mind, the questions it posed seemed unanswerable without knowing more about the human mind. How could a novelist know so much about the workings of the psyche, about questions of reality, sanity and judgement? Having always – to my shame – found the nineteenth-century writers impenetrable up to this point, I now felt that understanding a country's culture and language was nowhere near enough to fathom the universal themes raised by this book. This sense of a gap in my knowledge stayed with me as I graduated and began working in London.

Two years on, I decided to study psychology; a degree in Russian not proving enough to help me decide what I really wanted to do in my career. I was working happily as an administrator at the School of Slavonic and East European Studies at University College London by day while studying Psychology next door at Birkbeck College by night. If I thought this would help me understand more about the Russian masters, I was wrong. Undergraduate Psychology involves scientific exploration, statistics and brain processes that are far removed from the more indulgent psychoanalytic theory I had in mind.

When I saw a poster advertising a degree in Forensic Psychology, I realised I had found what I really wanted to do. A Masters at Surrey and subsequently three years of research at Liverpool allowed me to merge my relationship with Russia and my new-found love of Psychology. Sure enough, the first book on Surrey's reading list for my MSc was *Crime and Punishment*. I had come full circle.

Investigative Psychology is the application of scientific psychology to crime and the investigation of crime. It tries to apply science and rigour to the often intuitive field of offender profiling. Exploring the styles and patterns of the activities of criminals has led to the development of various systems of profiling, applying statistics to series of crimes. What better country to apply such techniques than Russia? The largest country in the world, spanning nine time-zones and with enough serial criminals to more than rival the United States of America. Those were the uncharted waters I sought.

This is where I found myself in 1999, embarking on a cross-cultural study of homicide. But trying to work out how to access data in Russia was proving impossible. Enter Dmitri Mironov, a young homicide detective who had established contact with my supervisor, having heard of his methods of profiling. Dmitri had studied Psychology at the Academy in the Ministry of Internal Affairs and his dissertation had focused on crime scenes, thus bringing him into contact with the police force, where he remained. He combined his academic life with his work as a detective, living in a small university hostel room and was rarely off-duty. Luckily for me, Dmitri had a fear of flying and on a policeman's wages he could only get as far as Poland on the train, so he was never going to make it over to the UK to expand his knowledge. I seized the opportunity to visit him in order to offer my help and to explore the possibility of gaining data for my research. In return I would teach the Moscow police what I knew of psychological profiling and about our latest software package for geographical profiling which could pinpoint the most likely location of an offender.

The largest federal police force in Russia was set up in 1772. At Petrovka 38, there are now 25 divisions responsible for various crimes and three divisions for the investigation of murder: contract killings; homicides and violent crimes. They even have a dedicated division for the murders of high-profile, well-known people such as journalists, politicians, oligarchs and so on. By 2002, one in five killings was a contract killing. The police, subsisting on meagre salaries of $90 (for a senior detective) a month, were riddled with corruption and one in four policemen was reported to be augmenting their income illegally.

The second division occupied a small office, also housing the squad investigating serial murders and child exploitation investigations. Since 2000, this squad has caught many serial killers, sexual offenders and those responsible for child pornography and other sexual offences against children. The detectives there are diligent and co-operate with international forces – with varying degrees of success.

I stayed with friends, Natasha and Yuri, whom I had met on my year in Russia during my degree. They were fearful of my involvement with the police, but humoured me, convinced that Dmitri had invited me solely because he wanted a British wife. Natasha would worry constantly about what I was doing at Petrovka and had a healthy fear of the police.

I met the chain-smoking Dmitri for the first time by a statue of Pushkin near to Pushkinskaia Metro station. We walked to Petrovka where he guided me past guards, through the creaking full-height turnstyle, past the immaculate flowerbeds and into the heart of Petrovka 38.

I was introduced to a small group of men who viewed me with varying degrees of interest – some giggling young detectives and some older, clichéd, drink-hardened detectives, who could have stepped out of a gritty crime drama. It was a male-dominated environment suddenly interrupted by a young British woman with slightly rusty and inadequate Russian (my degree didn't teach me serial killer vocab), anxious to make a good impression. What on earth would I have to teach these people?

I handed over the bottle of Johnny Walker Dmitri had requested I bring over with me (I later realised that I could have bought it more cheaply in this new Russia, which was so unfamiliar to my 1990s' version, in which vodka was the only alcohol on sale) and they put it away in the mini-fridge next to the antique, Soviet green safe where they kept their guns and bullets. An old television linked to a video recorder was perched on the safe.

The office was littered with papers stacked on two old sofas, ageing computers and piles of unpleasant photographs of crime scenes. Dmitri shared it with a colleague, who handed me a pile of indecent photographs to leaf through while I settled in to talk to Dmitri about how we might work together. On the noticeboard were photos of Andrei Chikatillo, Russia's most famous serial killer, alongside various other crime scene photos.

That afternoon, I sat down under the scrutiny of Dmitri and a few colleagues, to be shown some videos. Anyone who has spent much time in the former Soviet Union has learned not to be too surprised by anything that happens, but I barely managed to conceal my horror on being shown the films made by serial killer Anatoly Yemelianovich Slivko, who killed seven and tortured many more young boys between 1964 and 1985 in the North Caucasus. They showed me over an hour of the killer's own footage, followed by police footage of the victims' relatives and judges visiting the crime scenes. The film ended with Slivko himself being taken back to the burial sites on a remote island near the Caucasus – he hadn't been able to remember where he had buried all his victims. The film of him in court was equally disturbing: a broken man rocking back and forth in the dock. We discussed the psychological make-up of a man who could do such unspeakable things. As I didn't run screaming from the stifling hot room, I presumably passed the test and was accepted into the office. But those images stayed with me and I won't forget the horror and nausea I felt on watching them.

There was a lot of humour in the department despite the grimness of the work. I remember fondly a younger detective fetching us ice creams almost daily, bringing some of the carefree street-life of the Moscow summer into the sweltering office. When they weren't showing me horrendous videos, the television was tuned to the Crime Channel. One afternoon, I wrote in my diary how I was trying to read through files, but all I could hear was laughter as one of the detectives played a World War III computer game. How the totally serious Dmitri managed to catch offenders was beyond me. At the end of each day, the detectives would replace or retrieve their guns kept in the safe, and leave. There was a moment of total slapstick one day when a box of bullets spilt and bullets skidded all over the floor. The room was filled with giggling men crawling on all fours trying to retrieve them all.

We installed the software I brought from Liverpool and used it to analyse some crimes that were taking place at the time in Moscow. We managed to pinpoint where the killer was likely to be based using statistical analysis of distance from the site of the body. An offender's base is likely to be defined by the location of his or her crimes. Using maps to chart criminals' movements enables investigations to home in on likely offenders in the correct areas. We tried it out on a number of solved cases with some degree of accuracy and tried to help solve a series of five linked murders of women. I never knew if that was any help – the program suggested he lived in a cemetery.

This work was fascinating, and for me a great way to combine all my experiences into one. I also learned much about detectives in Russia. Some would abuse their position, take bribes or masquerade as traffic police to take on the spot fines. Putin, of course, has promised to clear all this up. My experience however, was of a group of incredibly dedicated young men, passionate about catching the perpetrators of abuse and murder, but also able to have fun and spend time to talk to an itinerant student from privileged England.

On my final morning in Moscow, I slept in after a vodka-fuelled farewell dinner with my old friends. At 6.30am, Dmitri and the ice cream detective, whose name I never knew, collected me in a police car and drove at 140km an hour through red lights to get me to the airport in time. They then accompanied me through Customs and waved me off through Passport Control.

My studies in Moscow and Liverpool had taught me that it might be exciting catching killers and glorifying their stories, but the reality was more sobering: the men I met in Moscow cared deeply about innocent victims, particularly – in Dmitri's case – those who were children.

Returning to the UK and re-reading *Crime and Punishment*, I started to question the direction I was taking in investigative psychology. What I was really interested in was helping people to come to terms with what caused them to take extreme measures and then to be racked with remorse, guilt and shame, or not as the case may be. No killer I have ever read about or encountered had a decent childhood: most, if not all, experienced some form of abuse or neglect as a child.

Shortly after my return to Liverpool, I embarked on a Doctorate in Clinical Psychology. I now work in the National Health Service as a Clinical Psychologist providing assessments, psychological therapy and consultation to people with acute mental health problems. I also provide expert witness reports and independent psychotherapy outside of the NHS. I have moved away from my Russian roots, but am occasionally reminded of my past life when someone from Eastern Europe is admitted to the hospital I work in. I happily continued like this until early 2012. Since then, calls have begun to come in from Russian nationals in the UK who require psychological intervention or psychological assessment reports for court proceedings, but whose English is poor or non-existent. Finally able to bring my two passions together, I am beginning to brush up my Russian language again to start out on a new chapter in my life – once again combining a love for Russian with psychology.

Marion Bates studied Russian at the University of Nottingham between 1989 and 1993, spending her year abroad in Kiev and Moscow. After graduation, she worked at the School of Slavonic and East European Studies at the University of London while also studying Psychology at Birkbeck College. She took an MSc in Forensic Psychology at Surrey University and became a researcher at the University of Liverpool's Centre for Investigative Psychology. During this time, she travelled to Moscow, helping homicide detectives working with serial crime. Marion received her Doctorate in Clinical Psychology from Liverpool University in 2007 and moved to London to work in North East London NHS Foundation Trust with people with Personality Disorder and other mental health difficulties. She has recently revived her Russian language skills in her private practice by carrying out court reports and psychotherapy with people from Russia and Eastern Europe. Marion lives in London, juggling work commitments with three children.

First day of the pea harvesting season. Combine harvesters supplied by the USA at the Ukraine–Moldovan border.

The last tour: Will Stamper (second left) with the British Military Mission at the Glienicke Bridge, Berlin

New friends. Will Stamper finds common cause with Soviet troops after the Berlin Wall is breached.

Vladimir Voinovich painted this portrait and entitled it 'The Englishwoman Rachel Farmer at the Russian fish market'.

...and here is the artist eating dried salted Russian fish, vobla, to celebrate the Grimsby fish project

A one-eyed citizen of St Petersburg. Pirate, the cat.

Inside Ulitsa Petrovka 38. Marion Bates and Dmitri Mironov, a homicide detective.

Rod Thornton (left) helps clear mines near Turbe, Bosnia, April 1993

UN tanks try to force a way through to besieged areas in Bosnia, 1993.

A teacher in Kosovo who served 11 years of a 15-year sentence for two blood feud killings. His nephews, although unborn at the time, could not attend school for fear of reprisals and were taught at home.

Distant view across the lake of the Solovki fortress/prison/monastery.

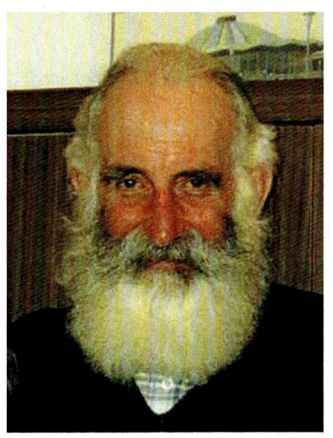

John Butler in Russia in the early 1990s.

Kazakh village familiar to Rachel Farmer from her business visits.

John Culley on his first trip to Russia, with his aunt in 1974.

Promotional brochure for the guided tour he led in 1980.

A funny old game: the St Petersburg White Knights rugby XV prepare for their inaugural match in 1994. Daniel Kearvell (front centre) launched the team, which is still playing in Russian leagues today.

Staying alive in the siege of Sarajevo

Rod Thornton *was part of a British army contingent sent to protect fuel supplies in Bosnia. As the mission expanded, his small band was caught up in dangerous political games*

The Siege of Sarajevo was the longest siege of a capital city in the history of modern warfare. The siege lasted three times longer than the Siege of Stalingrad and a year longer than the Siege of Leningrad. It is estimated that 11,000 civilians were killed or went missing in the city, including over 1,500 children.

I was sent from Vitez to Sarajevo in December of 1992 when Sarajevo was at the centre of the world's attention. It was a city under siege; cut off and bombarded by Serb guns. It had no power and a limited supply of drinking water and food. Slowly, inexorably, the daily shelling was reducing parts of Sarajevo to rubble. The UN had a presence in the city and it was doing its best to alleviate the suffering and to bring in aid; either through the occasional land convoy or via the more high-profile airlift.

During the six months I had previously spent in Sarajevo as a student, I can't say that I had a great time. The fun bit was getting there – driving across Europe in my little Ford Fiesta. Once I reached Sarajevo, though, it all went pear-shaped. I parked the car up the night I got there and, in a huge snowstorm, went off to find somewhere to stay. The next morning I went back to my car and found that all my possessions – for a six months' stay – had been stolen. Welcome to Sarajevo.

That was disturbing enough. But the strange thing was that the thieves had taken everything except the only items that were worth anything – my skis. They had been left in the car. It did not make sense. Why would anyone steal boxes of books weighing many kilograms and leave the skis? Given that I was now without clothes, bedding and books, I was forced to drive all the way back to the UK to get more of everything. Replete with all the necessaries, I then drove all the way back to Sarajevo.

Sarajevo had its problems even then. The worst thing was the pollution; the mountains surrounding the city on three sides form a bowl that traps car exhaust and factory fumes. And then there was the coming war. In the city there were many who felt a sense of hatred towards those not of their faith; and there were many more living in fear of where such a hatred would lead. A sense of dread hung over the city like the grey cloud of pollution.

Being in Sarajevo, I was reminded of the stories of Ivo Andrić. His Nobel Prize-winning books about life in Bosnia under Ottoman rule also carried an undercurrent of impending dread; of the inevitability of ethnic conflict. He understood the complicated politics and sociology of a region that had to cope with the misfortune of being at the juncture of three major religions. Sarajevo was not a comfortable place to be.

And then there was the music. In the normal run of things, my musical tastes could be described as quite eclectic. Bosnian music, however, had a character all of its own that my eclecticism did not cover. It can only be described as a sort of screechy folk-wailing garnished with a dash of white noise. It used to drive me mad when my fellow students played in it the accommodation block. And they played it *loud*. Bosnians never go in for half measures.

I was the only Westerner – as far as I could tell – resident in Sarajevo. I kind of dropped out: I did not attend many lectures; I also spent little time in my room since I had to share it with a rather creepy and suspiciously long-in-the-tooth medical student from Syria. He was no fun. So I was out all the time doing my own thing around the city and its environs. I loved it. I would climb the local hills and mountains; I would explore every Old Town back alley and I would lap up the fascinating history of this city that was not quite Europe and not quite Asia. I would soak up the vast range of architectural styles – from the magnificence of the Austro-Hungarian to the garishness of the Modernist. Thanks to the wonders of the socialist system, I managed to watch just about every opera that had ever been written for a ridiculously cheap price in the city's wonderfully ornate opera house. I also went to the cinema a lot.

Little did I realize, though, that my constant motion around the city was causing some consternation. Years later, an officer in the British Army was given access to the records of the Sarajevo branch of what had been, in 1991, the Yugoslav domestic intelligence service. They had a file on me. Apparently, I had been followed around by them for the whole six months. They did not, however, have much to say in my file, apart from 'he went to the cinema a lot'. That was a fair summary.

And now, in December 1992, I was back in Sarajevo. In terms of the UN troop presence, the French ruled Sarajevo. France had decided, a few months earlier, that if it were going to send its soldiers into Bosnia then it was going to send them to a place where the whole world could see them. The French wanted to be high-profile. Hence, they were in Sarajevo; the capital, and the symbol of Bosnia's suffering and the centre of the world's attention. The British government was quite happy to leave the French to it – French troops were dying every week in Sarajevo and the public popularity of the then-prime minister, John Major, would have suffered if he had sent British troops into harm's way. Our boys, the thinking ran, were much better off out in the sticks in Vitez where things were less hectic.

But that did not stop me and twelve colleagues coming to the city. We came in four tracked armoured personnel carriers (APCs look like tanks, but without the big gun). Our little band was commanded by a colour sergeant – CSgt Oram – and below him there was another sergeant. There was no officer with us. I was just along to interpret, nothing more. That was the best thing about being the interpreter: I had no responsibilities and no-one really ever gave me any orders. It was all very un-Army like.

Our mission was to escort British Army Logistics Corps diesel fuel tankers into and out of the city. These tankers were the idea of the British government's Overseas Development Agency (ODA) – or DfID as it is now. Someone, somewhere in Whitehall had decided that the UK should at least be seen to be doing something for the city and these fuel deliveries were to be it. The fuel was needed to keep the hospitals running and to power essential pieces of machinery such as the pumps at one of the local breweries. The pumps would provide pressure to water stand-pipes in various parts of the city. It was felt that the tanker trucks, which came in twice a week, should be escorted in and out by British troops and not left to the tender mercies of the French. It was also felt these troops should live in the city and know their way around it. We were the only British soldiers at that time in Sarajevo and it was to be a year or more later, after the siege had been well-nigh lifted, before any other British soldiers came anywhere near to living in Sarajevo.

But it was tricky: the French, *naturellement*, did not want the thirteen of us in Sarajevo and the British government didn't really want us there either. Diplomacy was thus called for. This was stressed in the briefing we were given before going into the city: 'Don't upset the French, keep a low-profile. And...oh yes... Don't upset the French.' We also needed to be plausibly deniable; and we were. John Major was able to say to the media, in that winter of 1992-93, that there were *no British troops serving in Sarajevo*.

As we drove down from Vitez and into the city on that first day, I couldn't resist a peek. I was sitting on my own in the back of CSgt Oram's command vehicle and the mortar hatches were open. These hatches are present on all APCs and can open out to allow mortars to be fired from the back or allow troops to stand up and fire out if needs be. I should have kept my head well down below the level of these open hatches so that it didn't get taken off by one of Sarajevo's local snipers. But I hadn't seen the city for such a long time and its destruction had been constantly in the news back home: I had to have a look.

The route taken into the city, instead of being the one I was used to (a turn-off from the motorway and straight down Marshal Tito Boulevard into the centre), was now a more circuitous route through a housing estate that skirted the airport. Marshal Tito had been blocked and mined.

All the houses that I could see in this suburban estate were burnt out, as were the bright-yellow 1980s blocks of flats that faced onto the airport. These were now mere blackened six-storey shells. All around the airport perimeter I could see that the French were building a huge earthen bank to protect airport workers from snipers hidden in the surrounding deserted buildings. The bank was like some massive First World War fortification. Building it, I was later to learn, would cost the French, on average, one man to a sniper every week. Further on, and having passed the airport, I could see a smashed and sorry-looking T-62[6] lying impotently – gun pointing skyward – in a roadside ditch. Trench systems and gun emplacements were everywhere. On my right, I caught a glimpse of a house I remembered. Emblazoned in huge blue letters across its front were still the evocative and now slightly comical words, *'Tito, volimo te!'* – 'Tito, we love you!' Bullets began to ping off the sides of the vehicle. I got my head down. Welcome back to Sarajevo.

We pulled up in the car park of the PTT building. This had once been the city's main post office. It was on Marshal Tito about two kilometres from the city centre and three from the airport. It was now the French army's headquarters and was to be our new home. The PTT was a fairly new and quite large three-storey structure. I had posted parcels from here when I was a student. The block of flats that had been my old student accommodation was just opposite on the other side of the boulevard. It was now totally gutted and every window had been blown in by explosions. As I looked back at my old home from that car park my heart

---

[6] A Soviet-era battle tank

sank. I remembered all the good—- and bad – times I had spent there and all the good – and bad – people I had met. Where the hell were they now? I particularly recall a Zimbabwean friend of mine. We had bonded because we, for some reason, had more in common with each other than we had with the 'weird' Bosnians around us. He had been studying dentistry at Sarajevo University and half of his room-space, I remember, was taken up with a huge dentist's chair he had acquired. He was going to take it back with him to Zimbabwe when he graduated. You just couldn't get them in his homeland, apparently. When we used to talk to each other across his tiny room we could not actually see each other because this gargantuan chair would always be between us. I wondered where he was now. And where the hell, I also wondered, was that bloody chair?

The standard of our accommodation in the PTT was basic. Even the most disingenuous of estate agents could not have put a positive spin on it. The building itself was obviously not in an attractive location and had no pleasant views. Indeed, for us thirteen British soldiers, there were no views at all. The French – bless 'em – put their beloved British guests in the one place for which they had no use: the PTT's basement nuclear bunker. This consisted of a large subterranean room with about twenty metal bunk beds, a bank vault-style door and no air. Air, apparently, was not standard. If you wanted air you had to go somewhere else. Of course, any self-respecting estate agent would have mentioned the positives – such as the safety facilities. We had our own bunker. However, nuclear shelters only really come into their own when there is a danger of actually getting nuked. And while the Serbs, Croats and Muslims had some serious issues, a nuclear exchange between them did not seem likely. So it was overkill on the protection front. Indeed, the PPT building itself was not even coming under that much fire, although people had been killed here and just outside. The shelling, this far out, was not as bad as down in the city centre and especially in the Old Town area.

We didn't have much interaction with the French. There was a sort of mutual suspicion. They were, after all, the British Army's traditional enemy (forget the Germans – those wars were just a couple of one-offs). We had an early run-in with them after we had started to fly the world's largest Union Jacks from our four vehicles as we drove around Sarajevo. We just couldn't manage to stay low-profile and British squaddies simply have no truck with diplomacy. We upset the French. Some French officer, in a fit of pique, fired off a complaint to someone somewhere important. We were then told by someone from somewhere important to put our flags away.

I tried to communicate occasionally in my schoolboy French, but it only went so far. I could talk about the 'pen of my aunt' but little else. However, *zut alors!,* the culinary fare offered by the French in the PTT was a revelation. This was not so much because of the food – we had expected that it would consist of salads and snails and not much else. No, the big surprise was the *wine*. In the middle of an operational zone, our French allies were quaffing alcohol; not only with their dinner, but at lunchtime as well. We discovered this astonishing fact the first time the thirteen of us lined up for a meal in the canteen with the French soldiers. The chefs were handing out bottles of wine – one between three – to people in the queue. How very civilized. How very *French*!

The British squaddie, of course, is only civilized – as far as drink is concerned – up to a certain point. To begin with, while the French may have perfected the high art of drinking in moderation, the British soldier is possessed of no such thing. If alcohol is to be drunk, the squaddie philosopher would venture, it should be drunk to excess. Otherwise, what's the point? So, after a quick discussion, we decided that one bottle of wine between three was a bit stingy. We hatched a plan that worked for many a meal hence: we would go up in threes to get our rabbit food and molluscs and the bottle of wine. Then we would mix up the threes and line up again. The French chefs never looked up to see who they were serving; they just handed over stuff willy-nilly. Another bottle of wine was thus procured. *Formidable, mes braves*!

Eight bottles of wine between thirteen of us was most effective. Tanked up, we were ready for absolutely anything in the afternoon. How simply dreadful you might think: pissed-up squaddies running around Sarajevo causing mayhem. But I tell you, those thirteen squaddies – pissed or sober – did more work in Sarajevo than the several hundred French troops had managed in all the months they had been there prior to our arrival.

Since we were only occupied with the tankers two days a week, we had another five to fill with something (there were no such things as days off – what would you do with one?). So we took the time to clear away all the wrecks of the shell-damaged tram cars that littered and blocked Marshal Tito. No French troops had seemingly wanted to risk moving them given the fire that was inevitable out there on the exposed highway. Amid sporadic shelling, mortaring and sniping, however, and over several days, our four tracked vehicles towed away all the tram wrecks. This meant that traffic could move freely up and down the road. This was a mixed blessing, though; yes, people could now venture out onto Marshal Tito and that did improve the transport situation, but it also meant that more people were now exposing themselves on that boulevard. Serb mortars subsequently took out many an unlucky *Zastava* or *Yugo* zooming down the road – a road that had become known to one and all as sniper alley.

Dealing with those trams made me a little sad. Many were the times as a student, that I had taken one on this same highway, either on journeys down to the city centre or up towards the outer suburb of Ilidža, with its parkland and lake and promise of escape from the city's rank pollution. Now the trams were just wrecks and objects to unceremoniously drag away.

Our sojourn with the French couldn't last, of course. A French sergeant-major, who was overseeing the PTT kitchen, wised up to our scam with the wine. We were rumbled. This, added to the fact that the French could never really get to grips with having British soldiers in *their* building, led to them asking us to leave. To ease the pain, though, they said that they had fixed us up with somewhere nice to live.

In fact, we were expelled down to the Old Town – the equivalent of a Second World War German soldier being sent to the Eastern Front – and told to report to the Egyptian barracks. The Egyptian element of the UN forces in Sarajevo occupied a five-storey building in the heart of the Old Town. It was a barrack-block built originally by the Austro-Hungarians and had been occupied most recently by troops from the Yugoslav army, the JNA (*Jugoslavenska Nationalnija Armija*). The building was set hard against a mountainside that rose steeply up to the commanding heights from where the Serb gunners were raining down all sorts of shot and shell. The front line was only 200 metres away.

Down there in the Old Town the walls of the mountains seem to press in from all sides and sunlight barely penetrated to warm the city's famous landmarks, which I had known well from my student days. Alongside the River Miljačka, and 100 metres from the barracks, was the Law Faculty of the university. It was there that I used to attend lectures (or rather was supposed to attend lectures). Also not far away and likewise set alongside the river was the beautifully ornate National Library – where I *did* read and study. Also on the riverside and midway between the library and the Law Faculty are the 'footmarks' of one Gavrilo Princip. Princip was the Black Hand terrorist who shot dead Archduke Franz Ferdinand on that July day in 1914 and precipitated the First World War. Into the pavement where he allegedly stood to fire his fatal shots is carved the shape of two feet. Above them is a plaque on a wall describing the action. The National Library also played a part in that particular drama. In 1914, the building was actually the Town Hall and Franz Ferdinand had just left it when he was attacked. Princip, once caught, was brought back into the same building. A year or so later – after I had left Bosnia - the library was hit by a mortar shell and gutted by fire. Most of Bosnia's literary treasures and artworks went up in smoke. The Bosnians had never bothered, despite all the dangers, to remove their precious artefacts.

We arrived at the Egyptian barracks in the middle of one of Sarajevo's monumental dumps of snow. A sentry sent us round to the rear of the building. At the back there was a narrow (fifteen-metre-wide) vehicle parking area between the rear of the barracks and the mountainside. Having parked and debussed, we moved at pace – mortar rounds were falling in the vicinity – to gain entry via the back door.

We went inside and were made very welcome by an Egyptian officer. He gave us a tour of the building. The cookhouse was on the ground floor and all the troops slept in the basement. Down there in the boiler rooms, within the dark recesses and amid miles of pipes, were set up hundreds of camp beds. It all looked deeply dingy and most uncomfortable. 'Why are there so many beds down here?' we asked.

There were a couple of hundred of Egyptians in the building and they all seemed to be living in the basement. Why weren't they spread out on the upper floors? 'No', said the officer, 'because of the shelling we all live down here in the cellar where it is safe.'

'Okay. So where do we sleep, then?'

'On the top floor.'

'On the top floor?'

'Top floor, yes. That is the only spare rooms we have.'

It transpired that the rooms at the top of the building were spare because the Egyptians – in mortal dread of the shelling – never dared venture up there. All the rooms on the other floors below the fifth were taken up by storerooms or, below them, by offices.

'You will be most comfortable up there. Lots of space.'

An estate agent would have had a hard job selling this one as well. While we now had more air, we also had some very noisy neighbours. And although we had better views than before we would rather not have been able to see, thank you very much, the shells and tracer bullets flying past the windows. However, the true negative for us was not so much being smack in the middle of war-zone central, but rather that we were such a *long way from the ground*. One of the most severe consequences of Sarajevo having no power was the fact that the lifts did not work. This meant that a fair proportion of the population, unable to climb flight upon flight of stairs within the innumerable blocks of flats, became housebound. And, if they became housebound, they could not go out to get water or food. Without help from neighbours, they could simply die.

We had much the same problem in the Egyptian barracks, although on a far less dramatic scale. While mobile generators kept the lights going, they could not provide enough power for the lifts. Thus all our kit had to be lugged to the top floor. This included weapons and ammunition, rations for several weeks (we dared not, despite the copious invites, eat in the Egyptians' restaurant) and all our water. And you have simply no idea how much water the average human needs in any one day – and how much it all weighs. There is water for drinking, for cooking, for washing and for flushing the toilet. It all adds up. And it had all to be brought up five flights of stairs in jerricans.

Eventually, though, we were all set up and settled into our new residence. There was no glass in the windows – it had long since been blown out by blasts – and the window spaces were covered by clear plastic sheeting. This kept the wind out, but not the cold. There was absolutely no furniture in the room, but we had brought our camp beds and sleeping bags and we used unopened ration boxes to create tables and chairs. It was like a camping expedition. We would cook communal meals – using food from our ration packs – on gas burners set up in the middle of the room. The fire hazard seemed inconsequential given the hazards that existed outside. At night, after a day's work, we would play board games and run card schools. We washed ourselves and our clothes when we could, but there was never any hot water. Even if someone did take the trouble to wash their nether garments in some chilly water, they would have to wait about a week before they would dry in the freezing room. Most of us had not had a shower since we had arrived in Bosnia some four months earlier and a flannel wash every now and again was the best that could be done. We all stank and we stank even more after three months in Sarajevo. But the fact that we were all equally malodorous meant that we didn't smell bad to each other.

There was, though, an immense amount of shelling. When bored of an evening, you could just sit by the window and watch the tracer and the impacts of shells, mortar rounds and anti-aircraft and heavy machine-gun bullets. Bonfire night had nothing on this. In that winter of 1992-93, at the height of the shelling of Sarajevo, there was an average of 700-800 explosions recorded every day by the UN authorities; the vast majority of them in the hours of darkness and within a mile of our building. On some days there would be over a thousand blasts and I still have a UN Daily Log for one such day. The blast waves of some of the explosions would push in or even tear the plastic sheets that covered the windows and occasionally there would be a thunderous drum-roll as the roof was struck by pieces of shrapnel. Each explosion would be preceded by a flash of light – day or night. And, as with lightning, there would always be some sort of time difference between flash and bang. Sometimes, though, the flash and bang came almost together. When they did, the noise would be less of a sound and more of a feeling, a sensation. A jack-hammer thump that shook everything in the room and everything in your body. If you had your mouth closed at the time of the thump, the pressure on your ears was immense. Still, to this day, I cannot see a camera-flash go off without bracing myself and waiting for the bang. Some things never leave you.

Sometimes the blasts would come sporadically, at other times they would come in intense barrages where explosions overlapped. It was scary. However, in that room we would all be doing our level best to remain calm while sitting chatting or huddled around our Monopoly board during the evening. (Scrabble was too cerebral and Risk was impossible since the tremors from the explosions blew the little armies all over the place. Huge dramas would then ensue over where they should be replaced – 'You did not have six armies on Argentina, no way!') Amid the mayhem outside, we would compete with one another to see who could come out with the most laid-back comment or droll remark. It was all an exercise in casual bravado and one-upmanship, but I am sure that everybody else's insides were churning just as wildly as mine.

It is remarkable, though, what the average human being becomes used to. After a while, the cacophony outside would just become part of the background noise; like the hum of an air conditioner or the tick of a loud clock. The explosions eventually came to be viewed by us as natural and undisturbing. We found we could all sleep through the noise of the explosions. I remember lying awake one night reading by torchlight and listening to a barrage that often shook the building and rattled every fixture and fitting within it, while the lads around me just snored on.

I also remember listening on one of the noisy evenings to the BBC World Service. On a news programme, it was comforting to hear it reiterated – by a government official in the House of Commons – that no-one should worry about British Army casualties amid the shelling of Sarajevo because there were no British Army personnel there. You just have no idea how disheartening it is for a soldier serving his country to hear that. Such is political expediency.

In that room at the top of the JNA barracks we had fun. That seems a strange thing to say, but squaddie humour always seems to become more profound the greater the degree of adversity faced. We blocked everything out by looking on the bright side. We weren't being disrespectful to the tragedy of the city; we were being defensive. Humour was our defence. We saw UN troops from other countries – Nordic and Dutch especially – getting so wound up by the situation that they could not operate effectively. They just did not have our peculiarly British coping strategy.

Every day for three months we would commute back to the PTT from the Egyptian barracks to get our tasking orders. We would drive out of the barracks' car park and then (unless there was a ceasefire) drive hell-for-leather to get across the bridge over the River Miljačka just opposite the National Library. This bridge was only a 100 or so metres from the barracks, but it was the only section on the early part of our route that was exposed to fire from the Serbs on the hill above us. Speed was vital so they had no time to react and get organised with their weapons. Once we had crossed the bridge and gone behind the line of buildings beginning with the National Library then we were pretty safe; until, that is, we emerged a kilometre or so later and were visible again from the hills at the beginning of the open Marshal Tito Boulevard. Occasionally, a bit of lazy mortaring would accompany us on our trips up the highway, but you would have to be very unlucky to be hit by a mortar in a moving vehicle. The main threat was the sniping from the blocks of flats on our left-hand side (on the way to the PTT). There would always be one or two bodies lying out here on the streets in the morning, victims of the snipers. Sometimes the bodies would be of young women incongruously dressed to the nines in the flashy *haute couture* style the women in Bosnia seemed to favour. Siege or no siege, they always wanted to look a million dollars. Fine. But you can't run very fast in a tight skirt and high heels; and there were places – exposed road junctions and the like – where you had better run fast. Some, sadly, did not run fast enough.

All of us by this time had become *blasé* about dead bodies. We had seen them just about every day out in Central Bosnia around Vitez and Travnik and now here in Sarajevo. In Central Bosnia I had spent much time arranging the exchange of dead bodies. All three sides wanted their own dead back in order to bury them in accordance with their religious practices. Thus one side would agree to exchange a dumper-truck full of those they had killed for a dumper-truck full of their dead comrades killed by the other side. A truck would arrive at the agreed exchange point, tip up and deposit its cargo in a huge heap. A truck from the other side would then do the same. Then all the bodies – some many weeks old – would be loaded onto the other truck and off they would drive. Everyone was happy. That was Bosnia. Ivo Andrić would understand.

Our main mission was, of course, the fuel deliveries. We would drive out of the PTT, down Marshal Tito, past the airport and out onto the main road to Kiseljak. In that town, and in a relatively peaceful area controlled by the Croats, was another UN HQ. Kiseljak was normally about an hour's drive away. At least it would have been about an hour if there had not been quite so many checkpoints on the way – Muslim, Serb and Croat – all of which would have one reason or another to detain us. There may have been a war in Bosnia, but Balkan bureaucracy was not a casualty of it. Pieces of paper were checked and rechecked and stamped in triplicate. Phone calls were made and verifications gone through. It all took so long.

Having picked up the two UN-white articulated tanker trucks in Kiseljak we would escort them back into the city. When we had the tankers with us and as we neared Sarajevo there was a distinct change in attitude at the checkpoints. The personnel there now went through their business with much more alacrity than they had on the way out. It was the tankers; they made juicy targets and no-one wanted them to hang around their checkpoint. And even though those who knew about such things kept saying that diesel fuel, if hit by any ordnance, would merely burn and not explode, they were not supplying absolute proof of this fact. So I had my doubts. This piece of science was also obviously lost on the owners of the local mortars. From the amount of fire the tankers attracted when stationary at checkpoints, the general assumption seemed to be that they must go up with quite a show. And if anyone – be they Serb, Muslim or Croat – could hit one of these tankers while it was parked at the checkpoint of their mortal enemies then it would be as if all their Christmases had come at once. You could almost hear their minds working: 'What kind of spectacular pyrotechnic show could we produce if we blow up one of those big white fuel tankers from the pesky UN at the checkpoint of those bastard Serb/Croat/Muslims [insert as required]?'

My morale was always in a bad place whenever we had to escort these tankers. It was the concept of being fried alive that didn't sit well. If your life ended in a bullet to the brain or a quick blast, then fair enough; but the thought of burning to death was truly scary.

Most panic vis-à-vis exploding fuel trucks was at the Serb checkpoint next to the airport. Where once bureaucracy had been king and paperwork pored over with a keen eye, now it was different. There was a 'get-those-fucking-things-away-from-my-checkpoint' hastiness. And what certainly put some vim into the pen-pushers was when they heard that unmistakable and blood-freezing sound – the plop of rounds being fired from a mortar tube. A mortar shell can be in the air for more than 30 seconds after being fired and so all soldiers know that they have roughly that amount of time to get the hell out of wherever they are before the rounds start landing. And, once a warning plop had set them off, the Serbs set world (or at least Balkan) records for document-checking and form-filling. Sometimes pieces of paper were even left unstamped. It was *that* serious.

The same scenario would be repeated a few hundred yards down the airport road at the Muslim checkpoint. A quick cursory glance at the paperwork and we were also waved through before everybody in *their* vicinity became a crispy critter.

As I mentioned, on tanker-less days we would do other jobs for the UN. We delivered aid both within the city and outside it. We tried to make absolutely sure we gave equal amounts to Serbs, Croats and Muslims (no-one, at this time, ever used the term 'Bosnjak'). Many of these extra jobs, however, often ended in huge frustration.

We would, for instance, go around to people in their blocks of flats and houses, offering sticky tape so that they could put it across their windows. This would go some way to preventing their windows being blown in by any nearby explosions. While the number of buildings being physically struck by shells was limited, the number of windows blown in by blast waves was great. This tape would not only prevent glass flying everywhere, it would also hold the glass in place in the window frames. It was especially vital here, in the bitter Bosnian winter, that the windows remained so that at least, to some degree, the cold could be kept out. And there was certainly no glass in the city to replace the windows once they'd gone. There was some plastic sheeting available but this was no use in keeping the cold out. Hypothermia could be just as great a killer as any piece of munition, especially for the elderly.

The taping of windows was, of course, common in Britain in both the First and Second World Wars. Virtually every building in the country had its windows taped – no matter how remote it was and no matter how unlikely it was that any passing Zeppelin or Dornier would drop something near it. But, incredibly, few of the people of Sarajevo could be bothered to shore up their windows. They just didn't get it. It was, for most of them, too much of an effort.

It was incredibly galling. Something so simple that could save lives and reduce suffering and yet the opportunity was not taken. But it was indicative of a certain *malaise* that seemed not uncommon in Bosnia and, indeed, elsewhere in Eastern Europe. It is that sense of Slavic fatalism; the idea that what will be, will be. It is an attitude that saps the will and prevents people taking even the most elementary of precautions and safety measures. In Bosnia, there were even people who just meekly marched away to be massacred. They did not even try to run away. There was a curious lack of will to *live*.

We were frustrated in other ways too. Every now and again we would escort groups of local workers around the city so they could carry out essential work on the water or sewage systems. The idea was that if any shelling started then the workers could shelter in the backs of our vehicles. Obviously, it would be all over if we took a direct hit, but we could offer protection from the more likely danger of flying shrapnel and debris. But even when the shells were landing a long way away, these workers would still insist on downing tools and crowding into the vehicles. Sometimes, despairing of their behaviour, we would even pick up their tools ourselves and start digging to give them encouragement to continue; but it was like pulling teeth. Moreover, they would work no more than six hours a day and wanted huge overtime payments from the UN to work more. The inhabitants of Sarajevo were desperate for water and wanted most of all to avoid the hideously dangerous queues at the standpipes. We ourselves had seen the results of a mortar shell landing among a queue at the brewery standpipe (any line of people visible from up on the hills would attract fire). Our tempers frayed with these lazy so-and-sos because we had no wish to see any more such carnage.

Sometimes the reasons for not restoring essential services were positively Machiavellian. On one occasion we were tasked with escorting five French army engineers whose job it was to fix some electricity pylons. Sarajevo had had no power for months. Things, however, were now looking up. Before I had been deployed into the city, I had accompanied Colonel Stewart in an attempt to get a coal-fired power station at Breža – some twenty or so kilometres north of Sarajevo – working. It appeared he must have been successful since the UN authorities now felt that if some damaged pylons could be fixed then there might be the chance to fire up some lights, heating and lifts in Sarajevo. The trouble was that several of these pylons were in the middle of the no-man's land between the front lines of the government forces (Muslim and Croat) and those of the Serbs up on the northern edge of the city. Apparently, though, the Serbs were amenable to allowing them to be fixed – many thousands of Serbs were, after all, also stuck in the city – and they agreed to suspend hostilities for a period. The government side likewise consented. And so we had ourselves another mission. We stuffed some nervous looking Frenchmen into the backs of our APCs and off we went.

The front lines were in a rural area of bare rolling hills. All the trees that I remembered from my student days had been taken for firewood. There was now a forest of tree stumps. As we approached the Muslim positions it became obvious that hostilities had not ceased. I could hear the sharp cracks of passing bullets even from inside the back of the APC. Once we had come to a halt, I opened the back door and saw the Muslim trenches and some bunkers away to the left. Still in the vehicle, I shouted above the din of battle to the trenches asking where the local commander was. The reply, from a disembodied voice whose owner kept his head well down below the trench parapet, was that I should head for the bunkers. I then ran from the APC and went, in a mad scramble, to the nearest of these.

'Where the fuck is the ceasefire?' I shouted in exasperation at someone who looked like a commander.

'*Nema problema*,' he shrugged, as if stopping a war was the easiest thing in the world. 'I will make some calls'.

He had used *that* phrase. He had said *nema problema* – 'no problem'. I always translated the phrase as 'we're all doomed'. Uttered by a Bosnian it more or less guaranteed that your problems were only just beginning. Never in any language has the conjunction of any two words resulted in a situation where the intended meaning is so far removed from the actual meaning.

I had, however, been a tad hasty this time. Sure enough, he did stop the war. After a few minutes, both his boys and those opposite in the Serb trenches had stopped firing. Incongruously, I could now suddenly hear birds twittering out here in the countryside. Spring was coming to Sarajevo.

I went back to the APC and told CSgt Oram what the situation was. With the cessation of hostilities we could now move the surface mines that blocked the track that led to the Serb lines. Our little convoy then set off past the Muslim front-line trenches and out into no-man's land. After about 300 metres we reached the Serb trenches. Once there, I dismounted and explained the situation to the Serbs. They had been warned off and were all smiles: 'You want to fix the pylons? Go on then, my friend. *Nema problema.*'

Oh, Lord.

Now we had to walk across the no-man's land to reach the pylons. The vehicles could not go out to them because both sides were reluctant for the UN vehicles to set off one of their precious (buried) land mines. They also said that there may be anti-personnel mines out there as well – but they were cheap; so neither Serb nor Muslim seemed to mind if we trod on one or two of them. I accompanied the French engineers out across a field of stubbly brown grass. The field was empty except for some patches of snow and a slightly bent pylon with its wires hanging limply downwards. It was 100 metres from the Serb lines and about 200 metres from the Muslim lines. The French engineers were not saying much and I had no conversation in me in any language. We were quieted by the sense of dread that seems to hang heavy in any no-man's land. I had crossed several back in Central Bosnia and it is a truly frightening experience. There is always the possibility of either side opening fire in order to create an incident that would blacken the name of their opponents – 'Shooting? It was them, not us!' But it was the mines that generated the most anxiety. All my concentration was on trying to walk without putting any pressure on the soles of my feet. It wasn't easy. It also wasn't easy when you were trying to look cool. You always – with such an international audience – had to give the impression (to the Serbs, to the Muslims but *especially* to the French) that you weren't scared. You walked carefully, but trying to do so as if you weren't – which is kind of tricky.

We reached the pylon. The head engineer took a look and indicated that it could be repaired. His schoolboy English explanation to me was then interrupted by the sound of bullets zinging off the metal-work of the pylon a little above our heads. We ran back to the Serb side, suddenly oblivious of everything, including mines and the need to be *insouciant*. While they may have been warning shots, you just never knew; better just to run – and fast. The firing had clearly come from the Muslim side. Once back at the Serb lines we quickly mounted up, bid the Serbs adieu and headed back along the track to the Muslim HQ bunker.

'Why are you firing? We are trying to get the power back on for *your* city.'

'New orders', said the local Muslim commander, meekly.

'Whose orders?'

'The government's.'

I didn't understand. One of the other officers in the bunker took me aside. His explanation went something like this: 'It's politics. The government needs Sarajevo without power. It needs it to be dark. It does not want normality. Normality means a lack of attention and a lack of world focus on Sarajevo. We need a city under duress, in pain, otherwise help from the rest of the world will diminish. We cannot let that happen.'

I stormed out and told CSgt Oram what the problem was and we were then off back down the hill and into the city. And that was that. No more attempts in my time in Sarajevo were made to restore the electricity supply. Indeed, it was almost eighteen months later that Sarajevo finally got some power back. Ivo Andrić would understand.

There was another incident that bore out the 'keeping Sarajevo in the world's eye' philosophy. It relates to Sarajevo being 'too quiet'.

The Serb shelling of the city stopped occasionally because of some temporary ceasefire. This made our lives much easier. It allowed us, for instance, to go outside into the small car park at the back of the Egyptian barracks and carry out some much-needed maintenance on the vehicles. Other Sarajevans took advantage as well: they came out to look for food or to queue up in safety at one of the water standpipes. But these ceasefires never lasted long; sometimes only a few hours, at best a few days. I became intrigued, however, by the fact that it was the forces of the *government (*those besieged) – and not the Serbs (the besiegers) – who re-started the bombardments. If we were anywhere near the Egyptian barracks - in the vehicle park or up in our room on the top floor - sometimes it was obvious that the initial firing was *outgoing*. And it would be coming from the building next to our barracks; another large Austro-Hungarian edifice that was, in fact, the headquarters for the government forces. Invisible to anyone outside the building – but impossible to disguise given the noise they made – heavy mortars had been set up in its inner courtyard. The rounds were aimed at the Serb suburb of Grbavica. This was an area of 1970s tower blocks about 2 kilometres down Marshal Tito, but still within besieged Sarajevo. Once these mortars kicked off it didn't take long before the Serbs responded from the hills. Ceasefire over and game on again.

But why would it be in the government's interest to end the ceasefires that were so helpful to the vast majority of Sarajevans – that is, those who were Muslim (mostly) and Croat? I was determined to find out. And so, one quiet morning as our vehicles were forming up outside the Egyptian barracks' front gate before setting off on that day's tasking, I asked one of the Muslim soldiers outside his HQ why it often seemed to be *his* side that broke the ceasefires. It was all about image, he shrugged. It was the same logic as with the power supply. The leverage that the government in Sarajevo could generate in international public opinion would only come if their city was being constantly oppressed, constantly shelled. The Serbs had to be forced into restarting their barrage.

It was that political expediency again. And it was dispiriting. Not only was such activity putting the lives of ordinary Sarajevans at risk, but also those of people from the international community who had to come to help. We were risking our lives. Indeed, many of the French and some Ukrainians and Egyptians were losing them. Moreover, wherever we went in Sarajevo – and in the rest of Bosnia – we as UN soldiers had to face a constant barrage of abuse. The whole situation, the whole war, according to Bosnians from Tuzla to Mostar; from Sarajevo to Doboj, and from government officials all the way down to lowly farmers, was the fault of the world community. It was the UN's fault and it was the fault of us, UN soldiers. Ivo Andrić would understand. Wouldn't he?

Rod Thornton studied Russian and Serbo-Croat at the University of Nottingham from 1988 to 1992. Previously he served for eight years in a British Army infantry regiment. He left as a sergeant. During his student year abroad, Rod spent six months at Sarajevo University. A few days later a conflict broke out in Slovenia that precipitated the Wars of Yugoslav succession, and it spread to Bosnia the next year. A UN 'peace support' mission was then established based in Sarajevo. On graduating Rod volunteered to rejoin the Army as an interpreter for the British forces who were about to be sent to join this UN operation. Thus in September 1992 he arrived with the first echelon of troops led by Colonel Bob Stewart (now an MP). A base was established at Vitez in Central Bosnia. Rod, who remained in Bosnia for a year, later came to be portrayed in a BBC mini-series called 'Warriors' where he was turned into a soldier of Polish descent – to explain why a British Army sergeant could speak Serbo-Croat!

Taking the bus

In an unbearably tense journey, **Vanessa Pupavac** *and her fellow passengers witness more of the Bosnian war than they bargain for*

The Bosnian War took place in Bosnia and Herzegovina between March 1 1992 and December 14 1995. The war was the consequence of the break-up of Yugoslavia and involved a great number of factions. The number of deaths is estimated at 100,000–110,000 and the number of people displaced at over 2.2 million, making it the most devastating conflict in Europe since the end of the Second World War.

Ko to tamo peva[7] is a classic Yugoslav film by Dušan Kovačević, which follows a group of incongruous characters on a long bus journey to the capital Belgrade in 1941 on the day before Nazi Germany began bombing Yugoslavia and the country was drawn into the Second World War. There is the pig merchant bus owner, his son and their pigs, the First World War veteran, the coughing hypochondriac, the singer, the hunter, the newly-married couple, the pro-German snob disdainful of his peasant surroundings, and the two gypsies, who are the only survivors when the bus is hit by a Luftwaffe shell. Anybody travelling on a long bus journey in the region is bound to observe their fellow passengers through the prism of that classic journey, which is at once comedy and social observation, but above all a humane celebration of life in its rich, stubborn, foolish diversity and frailty.

---

[7] 'Who's that singing over there?'

I found myself on one such journey in June 1995. I was a doctoral student researching nationalism and wanted to go to Republika Srpksa Krajina [RSK] – that is, into Croatian-Serb territory.

To get to RSK from Serbia, I needed to travel through Republika Srpska [RS] – that is, Bosnian-Serb held territory. The route followed the so-called Corridor. The Bosnian-Serb and Krajina-Serb territories were linked to Serbia by a narrow strip of land of near Brčko, known as the Posavina Corridor. At its narrowest point it was only two miles wide and vulnerable to attack. The Corridor had been fiercely fought over in 1992 as its ownership was crucial to the maintenance of RS's and RSK's core link to Serbia. The parts close to the front line frequently came under fire from the opposing Bosnian-Croat or Bosnian Muslim forces. When the fighting was intense, the route would be closed and vehicles would have to wait for hours, or even days, for military clearance to pass. Since Operation Flash in May 1995, when the Croatian forces took Slavonia from Croatian-Serb forces and Serbia did not intervene, there was a sense that RSK's days were numbered. Hence the Corridor had come under renewed pressure.

Hiring a car with or without a local driver was way beyond my student budget, even though strictly speaking I wasn't on a student budget, but a lecturer's salary. War had suspended the previous British Council scholarships and international sanctions meant that you couldn't get grants to study in Serbia. So I was lucky to have been offered a job teaching English at Novi Sad University to carry out my fieldwork. A lecturer's salary in wartime Serbia was around £100 per month – not easy for those who had to support a family. Since my salary only had to support me, it could just about stretch to a return bus ticket of around £25 to Knin, the capital of RSK. In any case, it was probably safer to be on a busy bus than in an isolated car if there were problems.

I set off early for the 6.30am bus from Belgrade bus station, armed with a rucksack, my passport and my invitation from the RSK Ministry of Education, as well as a large parcel of food. A food parcel with homemade cakes had been generously prepared for me by the 80-something-year-old writer Jara Ribnikar (1912-2007), with whom I was staying. Jara was a formidable character – she had been Tito's secretary in an earlier period. Yet she was very welcoming and patient towards the British students sent to her by her daughter Vladislava and son-in-law David Norris, my supervisors at the University of Nottingham.

As I waited at Belgrade bus station, I saw buses arriving from different towns. There was even a bus from Zagreb, the capital of Croatia. It was rather incongruous to think of a bus service going between two capitals (via Hungary) when the two countries were at war. But there it was, indistinguishable from all the other buses in the station. A young man hugged and kissed his girlfriend goodbye before she boarded the bus in a scene that could have taken place anywhere in the world. Nevertheless, seeing a man with an amputated leg balanced on crutches and the many women in black waiting to board, it was impossible to forget that this was war. The waiting passengers talked about rumours that the bus service between Belgrade and Zagreb might be stopped. The threat came not from the Croatian or Serbian authorities, but owing to the huge 500-Deutsche Mark tax that Hungarian border guards were demanding for every bus to go through their territory.

My first couple of attempts to travel to Knin proved a false start. Both times, the bus was cancelled because fighting forced the Corridor to close temporarily. But it was third time lucky and I set off, keeping my fingers crossed against the bus breaking down and against problems at the various police or military checkpoints along the route. The worn-out buses frequently broke down, not helped by the sanction-busting petrol from Romania, which was a substance of rather dubious provenance and was ruining everybody's engines.

Entering Bosnia

We entered Bosnia at Bosanska Raća and crossed the River Drina by an old single-track railway bridge. I did not dare look down as the overloaded bus squeezed past a lorry along the narrow dirt track on the very edge of the high railway embankment.

There were long queues either side of the border. Serbia had recently imposed sanctions on Republika Srpska in its efforts to please the international community and to try to relieve its international isolation. Every truck, bus and car had to be inspected. Trade was considerably reduced and there were serious shortages of goods within RS and RSK. RSK was particularly hit by these double international and national sanctions as its core essential links were via RS and Serbia. The price of black-market petrol in Serbia dropped to 1.5 dinar (30p) per litre as the number of illicit marketeers increased, while the price was 5-10 dinars (£1-£2) per litre in RSK and rising. The prices would have been higher still but few people could afford to buy anything anyway. The small border town of Bijeljina had become the centre for illicit trade between Serbia and RS. It was market day and the only lively town I saw during my fourteen-hour journey along the Corridor through Bosnia to Krajina.

I had happily blended in on the bus until we got to the border between Serbia and Bosnia. But at the border my passport revealed I was the only foreigner on the bus. It was an awkward time to be travelling through Bosnian-Serb territory. The Bosnian-Serb military, in anticipation of Western airstrikes, had taken Western peacekeepers hostage and handcuffed them to vital installations in Pale and elsewhere. The British Embassy was warning British citizens not to visit. There were few foreigners in Serbia or Bosnian-Serb territory, and even fewer in this period. So I stuck out like a sore thumb with my British passport showing my British maiden name printed inside.

With the tense atmosphere created by the hostage crisis and the recent Western airstrikes on Pale, I knew my presence and travel plans would arouse questions at checkpoints. Inevitably, at every checkpoint I would have to come off the bus and have my passport and documents checked and recorded. However, I wasn't worried about becoming a hostage. I considered the chance extremely remote. My young colleagues and I were convinced that the head of English at the Novi Sad University would never allow it. Not least there were masses of exam scripts needing to be marked on my return. So I was confident that even if it happened, I would soon be released back to my teaching commitments.

My main anxiety was therefore being allowed to travel through the checkpoints, rather than being detained. At the first border post, it was still early in the morning and I remember having to walk across a newly-washed floor and leaving conspicuous muddy footprints. I hoped this wasn't grounds for the sceptical official to decide I didn't have all the correct official authorisations and stamps, and send me back. I was very apologetic and was returned safely to the bus.

My foreign identity had now created curiosity among my fellow passengers, who had to wait patiently for my return at each checkpoint. What was I doing there? Where was I going? My English teaching at Novi Sad University persuaded them and proved to be my unofficial passport. From now on, at every checkpoint, a fellow passenger would vouch for me, although sometimes they had only travelled for a short part of the journey.

Into the Corridor

The passengers' questions were cut short by the shock of seeing the town of Brčko. Even those passengers who had made the journey several times were impacted by the sight of such destruction. Brčko is situated on the River Sava, whose course marks the border between Croatia and Bosnia. North of the River Sava were Croatian forces, while to the south were the Bosnian Muslim forces. Bosnian-Serbs held a narrow strip of land in between these two forces and only the northern part of Brčko, while the southern part of the town was under Bosnian Muslim control. The front line therefore ran through the town. Most of the houses along this narrow section were damaged by shell-fire. Few houses had windows but people were still living in them. Nearer the front line the houses were completely destroyed. Road signs warned you not to turn down certain streets to stop you straying onto the frontline.

The Croatian and Bosnian Muslim forces were trying to cut off this vital supply route from Serbia. The main road which borders onto Croatia had become too dangerous due to Croatian shelling so we had to travel along a pot-holed chalk track. All the traffic now had to go along this route, including tanks and heavy trucks. The pot-holes were a foot deep in places and for five miles the bus could not go more than five miles per hour. On the way back, the road had become even worse after heavy rainfalls.

Leaving Brčko, the road became better, but evidence of war was all around, especially in those areas where there had been fierce fighting to control the Corridor. The whole town of Derventa was bullet-scarred; not a single building appeared untouched. The outskirts of the town were deserted. Every house was barely a shell. Nearer the centre, people were somehow living in damaged blocks of flats where perhaps part of a wall had disappeared or just the balconies had been destroyed.

Other towns too along the route from Gradačac and Modrica to outside Prijedor, near the notorious Omarska and Trnjani, showed huge destruction from heavy fighting where every house had been damaged. But just as shocking was Banka Luka, where mosques had been destroyed. In some areas, among untouched houses, you could see isolated, bullet-marked, burnt-out and graffiti'd houses, which had obviously belonged to Bosnian-Croats or Bosnian Muslims in Bosnian-Serb neighbourhoods. The incredibly beautiful mountainous terrain from Sanki Most made the clusters of burnt-out houses of the mainly Muslim villages on the road to Petrovac seem particularly poignant. From Petrovac to Knin most of the villages are ethnically Serbian.

The passengers' tales

Life was evidently far from normal along the Corridor, and the passengers I encountered led far from normal lives.

For the first part of the journey, I was sitting next to a girl who lived with her boyfriend in Belgrade. Milica was going to visit her parents in Bosanski Petrovac. She had not seen them since the winter, as she could not afford the 120-dinar return fare (£20). Her 23-year-old brother was at the front and she was frightened for his safety. The other passengers were generally older, and were mostly women dressed in black.

Every so often along the route the coach stopped to pick up passengers and give lifts to soldiers. The Bosnian-Serb army did not have enough transport, so the coach drivers were instructed to allow soldiers to travel free to maintain the army's goodwill. There was now general mobilisation. A lot of the soldiers were young; they might have been going to Glastonbury with their long dishevelled hair, Nirvana T-shirts and rucksacks, but for the fact that they were carrying weapons.

Most of the passengers who got on the bus along the route in Bosnia also travelled free. People told me that soldiers were paid 30 dinars (£6) a month, but few women had work. Practically no factories were operating and salaries were not paid for months at a time. Many relied on remittances from family members abroad. There were frequent electricity and water cuts. All along the route I could see mainly women, often in black, or old men working in the fields.

Along with the general troubles, I encountered raw grief. One woman, picked up along the stretch of road between Sanski Most and Petrovac, was in tears after finding out her young son had just been killed at the front. Another passenger, who was also dressed in black, tried to comfort her.

But besides the grief, there was also joy in the form of the wedding party which got on at Kljuc. The groom's sister carried an enormous *gateau* which she had made for her brother's wedding. Since there was nowhere for her or her young daughter to sit, I offered to hold the cake. For hours I nervously balanced the delicate cake on my lap as the bus whizzed around mountain roads. The cake would have cost over two months' wages to make and I did not want to drop it. But as we moved towards Krajina, this light-hearted episode faded and the shadow of war loomed again.

Approach to Krajina

Towards Krajina, soldiers got on from the front line with stories of fierce ongoing battles. The atmosphere was very nervous from Kolonić to Grahovo. The local Bosnian-Serbian population feared that the territory was going to fall. Already it was within range of the Croatian heavy artillery. You could see refugees all along the route around Kolonić down to Drvar.

The coach picked up a young mother, her baby and her older daughter. They were returning home to Grahovo in a panic. She and her sister knew they had to flee but they did not want to go, nor did they know where to go. Nobody wants to become yet another refugee. A soldier in his mid-30s from Drvar told her to forget about worrying about having to sell or leave everything. He told her that she should just get out and save her and her children's lives. He told me he had a young daughter and an eight-month old baby. He too was returning to see how they were and organise them to flee to safer territory. He suffered from terrible headaches as he had been wounded in the neck. The doctors had said it was too dangerous to remove the bullet, so it was still there. Although he was wounded, he was considered fit to serve at the front as the defences were insecure and there was such a shortage of soldiers.

Finally I neared the RSK border. Things were tense at the checkpoint. Few passengers now remained on the bus. It was not certain whether civilian passengers, especially a foreigner, would be allowed to travel further. But the Bosnian-Serb soldier vouched for me and I was allowed to continue to Knin.

Return journey: mounting anxiety

A week later, on my return journey, the situation had already deteriorated along the Corridor. Grahovo was under attack from Croatian shells. Two houses were destroyed next to the bus stop just minutes before the bus arrived. The bus did not hang around and drove as fast as a dilapidated bus could out of Grahovo in the face of more shell attacks. We passengers spoke little as if, like the driver, we needed to focus on the road and not be distracted by chat. The mood was subdued and serious.

The more frequent shelling was forcing more people to think about leaving. Yet, despite the clear evidence of danger, there was still hesitancy. But just a few weeks later, there was a mass exodus of over 200,000 Krajina-Serbian refugees along the same route I had taken. Virtually everyone I had met or interviewed on my short trip to Knin – the education officials, the primary school teachers and pupils, the shopkeepers and the café owners – became refugees. My journey from Knin to Belgrade took approximately fourteen hours. But theirs, amid roads clogged up with other refugees, took a week. Among them was my future husband's 90-something grandmother with her small suitcase perched on a kindly neighbour's tractor. The neighbour's unselfish decision to find room for a frail, elderly woman, rather than extra precious possessions, is one of those unsung heroic decisions taken in the pressure of the moment that decide one's humanity. Such instances illustrate the philosopher Hannah Arendt's observation that those who prove most resistant to evil and selfishness in times of crisis are those who simply cannot live with themselves if they do bad things – rather than those who profess particular ethical, religious or political ideals.

Later I went to work as a translator at the International Criminal Tribunal in The Hague. The country's division was shocking for those of us who remembered better, peaceful times – I had been an exchange student in Sarajevo in the mid-1980s. The last gasps of the war in summer 1995 were brutal experiences for friends in Srebrenica, in Krajina and elsewhere. I was fortunate not to see the brutality of war directly, and only through the witness statements I translated. Fellow University of Nottingham students like Nick Stansfield and Rod Thornton, who worked as peacekeepers in Bosnia, came face-to-face with war's brutality. Rod was among British soldiers who had to gather the bodies in the infamous Ahmići massacre of April 1993, where over a hundred Bosnian Muslim villagers, including many women and children, were killed by Bosnian Croats. Rod was also among

British soldiers who, under fire, managed to put a tram back on its tracks in the besieged Sarajevo. Rod modestly attributes the feat to the support of the French troops' wine ration.

All of us former students became personally shaped by the war in some way. The suffering of refugees, in particular, I think made all of us more sensitive to questions of justice, more impatient with authority and perhaps more compelled to speak out against injustice than we might otherwise have been.

Postscript

Seventeen years have passed (at the time of writing, in April 2012) since that journey. While many houses have been rebuilt in the towns I passed through, the region remains impoverished and depopulated, especially in the rural areas. Consequently, some parts are very overgrown and not just where there are mine fields. Wolves, wild boar and even bears have become more established again in the region. Last August, we were walking in the mountains near Knin with a Croatian friend. We became disorientated by the overgrown woods and were pleased to reach a road. We were happily anticipating food and drink, when we suddenly realised we had somehow crossed over into Bosnia and were on the road to Grahovo. We almost wished we had been picked up by border guards, instead of facing the prospect of hours retracing our steps. Luckily we didn't encounter a bear or a wolf, though it might have made a good story for our son to tell at primary school.

Vanessa Pupavac studied Russian and Serbo-Croat at the University of Nottingham from 1983 to 1988. During her degree, she spent a year at the University of Sarajevo in 1986-1987. After her degree, she trained as a solicitor but returned to Nottingham to study a doctorate on Yugoslav self-determination politics. She also taught English at Novi Sad University, Yugoslavia and worked at the International Criminal Court for Former Yugoslavia in The Hague before being appointed as a lecturer in the School of Politics and International Relations at the University of Nottingham. She is author of Language Rights: From Free Speech to Linguistic Governance (2012)

Monitoring the media

Former journalist **Colin Davison** *became an expert observer of the East European media before and after Communism. His work revealed to the West the medieval practice of vendetta in Yugoslavia, where never-ending cycles of murder trapped hundreds of families in misery*

According to the Committee to Protect Journalists (CPJ), free media in a number of countries that once belonged to the former Soviet Union continue to decline. In Turkmenistan, the president personally approves the front pages of the major dailies and newscasters begin each broadcast with a pledge that their tongues will shrivel if their reports ever slander Turkmenistan, the flag or the president. Uzbekistan has instigated an 'informal system of state censorship', forcing foreign correspondents to leave the country and jailing some Uzbek journalists. In Belarus printing of independent newspapers has been stopped and journalists have been jailed for covering opposition rallies. The Russian Union of Journalists says 211 journalists have been killed in Russia since 1992.

THE clock moved slowly to 10.25, and the discussion moved more slowly still onto the tricky question of a local engineering dispute. Was it time, the brothers of Leeds Trades Council wanted to know (in 1972 there were no sisters), to send messages of fraternal solidarity, or merely of fraternal and moral support?

Was it time, my colleagues at the press table wanted to know after three hours of interminable debate, for a pint before last orders were called at the City Vaults next door? It was the call to the bar (well, the pub to be more precise) that decided me – and it changed my life.

After graduating from the Department of Slavonic Studies, Nottingham, in 1969, I had been working as a reporter on the *Yorkshire Evening Post*, and hoped for a job as a foreign correspondent. A few weeks before, the British Council had offered me a one-year scholarship to Belgrade. I knew no-one there, the stipend was meagre, and my recollection of Serbo-Croat was largely confined to the opening chapter of Professor Monica Partridge's[8] practical grammar and reader, in which newcomers to the land and language were given a helpful phrase – should conversation turn that way – that Diocletian had been a Roman emperor.

On the other hand, I was on only a fortnight's notice and had that time owing in holidays. I could in effect resign with immediate effect, but was undecided what to do – until that debate that went on and on. 'Sod this,' I told my mate from the *Yorkshire Post*. 'I'm off to Yugoslavia.'

A few days later, on a journey largely following the route of the Orient Express but with little of its romantic appeal, I was already learning something of the peculiarities of a social system that seemed to have grown and thrived in the large crack that opened between Eastern and Western Europe. The train was filled mainly by returning Yugoslav migrant workers, their wallets stuffed with Deutschmarks, which a surprising number were ready to share – with heart-breaking enthusiasm – with the pairs of tricksters working the shell trick along the corridor.

Elsewhere, the large bundles tied with string, stuffed onto parcel shelves or under seats, bore witness to a strange international trade for which the train provided commercial passage. It was a three-way enterprise: the packages into the

---

[8] Head of the Department of Slavonic Studies at the University of Nottingham, 1969-82.

country contained western designer-label jeans for the fashion-conscious of Zagreb and Belgrade, where they could be traded for soft-porn magazines that were then smuggled – for a small consideration at the border – into Bulgaria. With little there that might appeal to Italian shoppers, the enterprising traders filled their bags with vegetables for the return journey. I never discovered whether Communist cabbages were officially regarded as contraband in Trieste.

The official purpose of the scholarship was to study the Yugoslav press, an activity by which I hoped to make contacts in the country and join the foreign staff of a press agency without the necessity of having to serve an apprenticeship as a sub-editor back on the home desk in the UK. The bursary provided free weekly language lessons, shared with an adventurous company of Scandinavians, Germans and French, and a couple of taciturn Russians, whose dress and demeanour resembled that of Mormons fallen into the second circle of Dante's *Inferno*. It also brought registration at the University of Belgrade, in my case in the politics faculty, under the tutelage of the excellent Sergej Lukić, whose colourful career had included time on *The Daily Mirror* in London. Through him I learned something of the eccentricities of the Yugoslav media, its edgy liberality, the industrial freedoms and the sheer irritation of its self-managing regulation.

Lukić was then sports editor of the respected political weekly *Nin*, a lively and relatively outspoken magazine published by the daily newspaper *Politika*, organ of the Socialist Alliance, which was essentially a front organisation of the Communist League.

However, he had not always been concerned with the fortunes of *Crvena Zvezda* football club, *Partizan*, or of the national basketball team. As a political columnist he had taken advantage of more tolerant times to express, moderately and not without encouragement, ideas that had proved a little too inflammatory. His banishment had been to the sports desk. Other offenders were serving terms of pleasant probation in *Politika*'s more distant offices. Its correspondents in London, Paris and other capitals were former editors or commentators whose writing had similarly caused upset. But to my knowledge, none was ever fired, and now free from the fear of the unpredictable retribution that they might have endured in an uncertain environment at home, they could comment with little restraint on how politicians dealt with recognisably similar issues abroad. It seemed, even then, an attractive if unconventional strategy for achieving the most desirable appointments in the press.

'We don't have political democracy. Instead we have industrial democracy,' a senior regional politician told me with some pride. It did seem to me, a former trainee reporter with more experience of union involvement than of party political activity, a worthy achievement. But as the months passed, the frustrations of working within a system in which the employee was also employer and virtually unsackable became more apparent. Much of my time in Belgrade was spent in the libraries of its national newspapers, largely undisturbed by the intrusion of journalists actually employed there. Yet, I discovered, there was considerable interaction between the library staff and journalists in other ways. For each department negotiated its terms of pay and conditions with other groups of workers within the organisation, as did the printers, advertising staff and even the managing director. It was a lengthy business. I had left the seemingly endless deliberations of Leeds Trades Council for the land of *mitingovanje,* in which the normal running of every enterprise was disrupted by seemingly endless consultations.

One of the delights of Yugoslavia in the autumn of 1972 was to be one of the few foreign journalists in the capital of a country acutely aware of being under scrutiny from East and West. International conferences convened on the delightful Adriatic coast to debate and generally to congratulate their hosts on the achievements of self-management and express faith in the future development of a third way in the genealogy of political evolution. One of my fellow tenants renting a splendid house in uphill, upmarket Dedinje, the Belgrade suburb of choice for Tito and the reputed CIA bureau chief down the road, was a Harvard student writing a paper on the development of democracy within one-party states. Thinking it would be a good idea to get the views of the head of the government, he telephoned the prime minister's office to request an interview with a senior official. When could he come, he was asked? He saw the PM within the week.

But the situation was about to change. At about this time, Tito published what became known as his letter to the nation, *Titovo pismo*, expressing anxiety about the effects of excessive liberalisation on the integrity of the national federation. The accelerating economic development of the republics of Slovenia and Croatia in the north-west could strain relations with the dependent southern regions of Kosovo and Macedonia, leading potentially to the resurrection of older, ethnic resentments. That painfully prescient message, even if not explicit, changed the political climate instantly. Visiting academics no longer found doors open. They came, spoke to Tito's disgraced former deputy Milovan Djilas – now living quietly and impotently in his unremarkable flat not far from that of his old nemesis Aleksandar Ranković, reportedly sacked for bugging Tito's home – and left without finding a single government official willing to talk to them.

My own achievements were less glorious than those of my flat-mate. The subject of my research had been somewhat inaccurately translated as Žurnalistika, as a result of which I had been provisionally enrolled in classes to learn the basic elements of reporting. As I had been working as a journalist for a couple of years, it was agreed that I might be excused and as a consequence became a student without studies. What I failed to learn about socialist realism in reporting, however, was more than repaid by the insight I gained into the daily lives of the Belgrade middle class – as represented by four students to whom I taught English in their homes for the next year. Among them was a disillusioned executive of the state airline JAT ('Just Any Time', he said it meant, and drew the curtains before whispering about the informers living in his Novi Beograd apartment block), and a determinedly anti-Communist former lawyer. At his home in a tree-lined suburb, Antun would greet me with a glass of *Dingač*, the red wine of his native Dalmatia, play records of Maria Callas, and talk of his naughty, youthful adventures in Rome's Via Veneto. He spoke also of how the whole house, not just the two small, over-furnished rooms in which he and his wife now lived, had once been his, until the end of the Second World War and the liberation of the city by the Partisans. Then people's commissars had inspected the property. Another family had been moved upstairs, another into his front rooms, the main entrance had been blocked off and he was ordered to build a side access for his own use.

In comparison with similar newspapers in Eastern Europe at the time, *Politika* was quite a lively publication. The same could not be said for *Borba*, the official organ of the Communist League, although it also published the more popular *Večerne Novosti* which maintained reader interest with a splattering of crime and stories of misfortune not dissimilar to that of a British regional newspaper. A series of reports of a particularly sensational murder that winter seized my attention as a subject for a feature for the British press. In southern Serbia, a young man on his way to join the army had been killed in a road accident involving two lorries. The victim's step-mother anonymously visited the home of the other driver, who had apparently been blameless in the tragedy, hired an assassin and arranged the murder not of the driver but of his eleven-year-old son. It was not the crime itself that became an object of terrible fascination, extraordinary though it was, but the code of vengeance from which it arose, and which survived in the most culturally backward regions of the country, in and around Montenegro, Kosovo and Macedonia.

The unwritten code, ascribed by Albanians to the medieval count Leke Dukadjini, who resisted Turkish invaders in the Northern Highlands of his country, demanded an eye for an eye, blood for blood, and not necessarily that of the perpetrator of the original crime. Close relatives of victims who failed to carry out their obligations were punished by social ostracism. Over the next few months I travelled to prisons to interview those who had. They included a former soldier who for years had been shamed by having the unwashed shirt of his murdered brother, still bearing its now-faded bloodstains, hung outside the door of his house on the anniversary of the original crime. Coffee was served to him under an arm as a sign of disrespect. No woman would associate with him. He eventually tracked down the killer, who had by then completed a prison sentence, in a fashionable Adriatic resort, shot him dead and immediately gave himself up to the police. 'Congratulate me, I have taken our family's blood,' he announced.

One of the most baleful consequences of feuds that could last many generations was the practice of voluntary home imprisonment by the family of a man guilty of murder, manslaughter or serious harm, even when adjudged to have acted in self-defence. There were, at the time, an estimated 1,000 families incarcerated behind the high perimeter walls of their communal homes, where no males over the age of puberty had ventured outside sometimes for years, partly from fear of vengeance, partly they told me out of respect for their enemies. Among those I visited, usually accompanied by one of the semi-official peace-makers who tried to arrange an end to enmities through the unofficial payment of blood money, was an extended family of fourteen souls in the miserable town of Suva Reka, Kosovo, where the boys had not attended school for six years. In Montenegro, I sat cross-legged in the main upper room of a similar fortified home, where the shutters were never opened, and only one dim candle burned. It was not only a matter of economy, explained the patriarch, a slight, prematurely aged man of 45 who had served six years for manslaughter. Their enemies, who had refused all peace proposals, might see them if a light showed through the wattle walls, he said.

Legislators faced difficulty in handling blood feud cases: such murders were the most corrosive of all crimes as they frequently led to a succession of killings, yet they tended to be carried out by those with no previous criminal convictions, driven by what they tragically regarded as a social duty. The law provided severe penalties for those who threatened to carry out retaliatory crimes so why, I wondered, were so many unable to leave their own homes for fear of revenge attacks? I found the head of the opposing clan in Suva Reka living in a decrepit house nearby that would clearly have benefited from the proceeds of a blood settlement. Why, I asked him, could his enemies not leave their house? 'They can come and go freely as they wish,' he said. 'Of course, they would not insult me by doing so. And, who knows, anyone can suffer an accident.'

Despite joining the news agency United Press International with a view to returning to Eastern Europe, I was to wait nearly twenty years before I was to work there again, under circumstances that could not have been more different. Following the fall of Communism in Hungary in 1990, each of the seventeen regional daily newspapers in that country was sold to foreign publishers, most of them to Swiss, Austrians and Germans, but one, *Kisalföld* in the most westerly region of the same name, was bought by the *Daily Mail* group whose proprietor, the late Lord Rothermere, had a sentimental attachment to the country. Back in 1920, his great uncle, Lord Northcliffe, had launched an unlikely campaign against the Treaty of Trianon, part of the settlement after the Great War. As a result of his campaign, 'Justice for the Hungarians,' residents of Sopron in the Kisalföld district had been allowed to decide their futures and voted to join an independent Hungary rather than remain in Austria. Northcliffe was feted and a street named after him in Budapest. He was even invited, it was said by the family, to become the new head of state – an honour which history showed he was wise to decline.

As editor of the West Country daily, *Western Morning News*, the closest equivalent title to *Kisalföld* owned by the *Mail*, I was invited to work with the local journalists as they prepared for the first time to face the wind of competition. Theirs had once been the only newspaper in the region. As it had been controlled by the Party its interpretation of the news was self-definitively true, so any other title would have been superfluous. As an editor accustomed to working within a commercial environment, and aware of the need to retain an audience attractive to advertisers, it was bemusing to discover that my opposite number could be fined by the old regime if his newspaper carried more than three per cent of advertising. With advertising taking up 60 per cent or more of regional newspapers at home, this was a luxury of which I could only dream.

But if the lack of advertising was surprising, what would have struck any journalist from Britain was the greater paucity of news. It was a situation encountered time and again when, years later, I was working as a consultant in Slovakia. *Kisalföld* had approximately the same number of staff as my own newspaper, yet the news room at its head office in Györ was almost devoid of reporters. Nor was anyone certain where the missing staff were. Some, it turned out, had taken part-time jobs elsewhere to supplement their salaries, but for most the explanation lay in the newspaper planning logbook that the deputy editor proudly displayed one Friday afternoon.

Almost every writing journalist was designated an editor, whose job it was to compose commentaries on his or her particular subject, be it politics, economic affairs, third world development (this on a medium-sized regional newspaper), or defence. The journalist alone decided what he would write about, which events he would cover – conferences in Venice, Vienna and Rome were strangely popular – and largely dictated in advance how much should get into the newspaper, and what its headline should be. Thus on that Friday, the deputy editor could show exactly what was likely to appear on each of the eight pages of the newspaper every day for the week ahead, even before the happenings they purportedly described had taken place.

In the weeks to come, one event did inconveniently intrude into this legacy of socialist planning. A mass grave had been uncovered containing the bodies of rebels executed after the 1956 uprising, and for the first time their identities had been confirmed. The story was momentous and the newspaper appropriately cleared its front page to give it extensive but by no means exhaustive coverage. Who had covered the story, I wanted to know, and how was it being developed? In its way, the editor's reply was also momentous. The newspaper had relied on a freelance, he explained, because none of its reporters were available. The editor did not stay long.

It was not that many of the journalists still supported the Communist ideology; more that the structures of the past were not easily adapted to the faster demands of a free market, into which new competitors, independent newspapers and press agencies, were moving rapidly. Having experienced life only in a highly-regulated environment, it was not surprising if some were slow to respond. Freedom, in those early days, seemed to promise a franchise for the individual to do as he or she pleased. Commentators would remain commentators, writing lengthy columns that were just as dull as before, but now expressing their own rather than the Party's prejudices. As a result, they confidently expected that soon they would be driving Mercedes.

Transformation did indeed come. Today the press in Hungary, the Czech Republic and Slovakia is as diverse as that of the UK. Mini-tabloids copied from German models have generated mass readerships, publications such as *Kisalföld* and *Pravda* in Bratislava have consolidated their positions in the middle markets, but only by reacting to what their readers wanted. Competition is tough but produces vibrant debate. Journalists, generally better educated than their British counterparts, are influential figures nationally and in their communities. Less beholden to old traditions, many embraced internet journalism more readily than inkies like me. With new presses and showpiece buildings that speak of their confident role in society, with changed working methods and processes of accountability, they clearly no longer want the services of this old newspaperman. It makes me feel rather proud.

Since retiring in 2006, Colin Davison has written a biography of a children's author, Through the Magic Door – Ursula Moray Williams, Gobbolino and the Little Wooden Horse (April 2011, Northumbria Press).

The ghost of St Petersburg past

Hannah Collins *took a step back in time when she went to stay in the antiquated apartment of a lonely, elderly lady*

St Petersburg was founded by Peter the Great in 1703. From 1713 to 1728 and from 1732 to 1918, St Petersburg was the Imperial capital of Russia. It is Russia's second-largest city after Moscow, with around 5 million inhabitants and is an important Russian port on the Baltic. In 1914, the name of the city was changed to Petrograd and then to Leningrad in 1924, five days after Lenin's death. In 1991, it became St Petersburg once again.

I'M surprised that I didn't hate her in the end, but either out of naivety, stupidity or some kind of misplaced affection, I became rather fond of her. Despite her faults, she instilled in me a feeling of both motherly warmth and anxiety that I had never experienced before.

    I remember when the cat followed me home. It was a poor scruffy thing, with lots of white fur (turned grey) and one closed eye. He followed me all the way into the grubby hallway of bare concrete, up the stairwells of the same material and to the door of Irina's flat. When I arrived at the flat, I was met with the same large grin and look of joy as this poor little fellow, except that to me she exclaimed 'Oh she's blonde!' and gave me a big hug. The cat got the honour of sitting on top of the washing machine in the bathroom.

She was a large woman with features that had aged in a way I'd never seen before. Her smile could fast turn into a grimace, but her mannerisms had a kind of tough love about them. I remember coming home one day to find Pirate (pronounced *pee-rat* in Russian; he was aptly named for his one eye) in the bath, looking half the cat he was before. She had decided it was high time he had a haircut and a bath, and the poor thing was screeching and looked a skinny mess. But I could see she enjoyed taking care of him. 'Don't worry, you're with me,' she kept saying to him with an air of loving emergency. She was enjoying herself. There was a strange medicinal smell in the bathroom, something familiar to me. I looked towards the bathroom shelf and noticed that my bottle of mouthwash had been entirely emptied. Pirate came out of there looking shiny and smelling curiously minty-fresh.

The hallway had a cupboard full of quaint tea cups and saucers, the kitchen dining table had old jam left in a bowl decorated with pictures of fake-looking flowers and there were teddy bears placed decoratively in the hallway in nativity-like fashion: teddies on sledges, teddies on tyres, teddies in bed, flowers 'tastefully' arranged next to teddies. My room was large and well-decorated – and although the decoration was clearly old, the room was incredibly well looked after. There was a striking picture on the wall, unexpected in the home of an elderly lady with decidedly conservative views. It was a portrait painting of a beautiful young woman with long, wavy, dark hair, wearing nothing but a pale green silk shirt which was unbuttoned and positioned so as not reveal all of her chest.

Despite her offbeat behaviour, there was an elegance about Irina; she took care of everything: her hair, her clothes, her make up and apartment equally. She had coats and jackets that she had kept for 30 years and brushed every day. Going outside with her felt, in a strange way, like a privilege and an event. She made a conscious effort to walk with a straight back and would smile and wave at the neighbours as she passed by in a regal way that was entirely new to me.

The neighbours were her enemies and her spies; all of them knew exactly what was going on in the area and I frequently received reports from Irina that the other women had seen me leaving the apartment without cleaning my boots. Although she partook in the monitoring, she told me that she despised the other women for doing so. Thanks to free calls to all apartments in the area, Irina's phone never stopped ringing with updates.

Over the five months that I lived with her, we came to know each other well. She told me a little about her past, when she lived on a large farm in Vladimir during Stalin's reign. Huge batches of soup cooked by her mother would last them for days. She remembered singing with her brothers – she had fond memories of this time and saw it as a better time; she seemed to glorify it, as if trying to make a point to me. She believed that I might become a spy or that people working at my university might be spies. She often cried about the Yeltsin era, a time when she was so poor she had to sell cigarettes from a cardboard box outside a metro station in St Petersburg; also about a time when she lived in a communal hall with her baby daughter (there was no mention of any husband). And I remember the morning Medvedev was elected, she woke me up and came into my room crying: 'Putin is in!', tears running down her face. She was overjoyed and that morning she sang the 1930s Russian classic 'Burnt by the Sun' to me with a brightly coloured headscarf on as if in the throes of euphoria. Sometimes I felt I was living in a past Russia and I felt guilty for regarding her as an anachronism.

She did, however, provide me with ample reason to ignore this guilt. She would tell me that I looked like a man one day and Barbie the next; she said I was like a prostitute for wanting to go to a restaurant with some friends; and she would not give me my own key to the apartment, frequently locking the door and leaving me in the house when she decided to go to the shop. Our conversations were another source of tension. According to her, homosexuals are not people and immigration is the source of all of England's problems; and she made very clear and unsettling distinctions between 'our' country and 'your' country.

Irina was very different from my own mother or, in fact, any mother I had ever met before. All I'd ever heard from my own mother was 'as long as you're happy'. Irina saw me as a work in progress (even though I was 21 and paying her enough money to rent the whole apartment) and some days it felt as if I was at some kind of finishing school. She wanted to brush my hair, told me how I should polish my boots and walk with a straight back, how to carry my bag, and even tried to set me up with a guy who worked in the local phone shop, assuring me that my own boyfriend would be living on the streets in no time (she'd seen a photograph of him and decided that he would amount to nothing). She told me that she had tried to find my diary (which luckily didn't exist) and I frequently noticed that things had been moved about my room. She also insisted that she come with me to buy my first gold necklace – something which seemed to be of great importance to her. She looked at me with such pride when I tried one on, as if I had suddenly morphed into a real woman before her eyes.

My going out always presented Irina with ethical and practical problems: would she be awake to let me in? Would I be home for dinner? Would I be taking drugs? Was I a prostitute? Her paranoia knew no bounds. Whenever I did manage to get out, I was scolded when I returned. She would pull the skin under her eyes and make impressions of my tired face over dinner and often there would be a token quote from her idol Sophia Loren on how to stay looking youthful.

Luckily, later on, I found I could take refuge at a friend's place whenever I went out for the evening. We frequently went to a café called *Stirka*; it was a very small, dark launderette-cum-café/bar and had the feel of a bar you might find in Berlin or Paris, with local artwork and photographic displays on the wall, live music and a piano. Most other cafés were overpriced Russian franchises which resembled Starbucks or Costa, where we had to pay the equivalent of five pounds for a coffee (I couldn't understand how the average person living in St Petersburg could afford even one of these Knickerbocker glory-style coffees). One evening we shared some drinks in *Stirka* with a guy named Mikhail and his friends. Mikhail's father wanted him to become a sailor, but he had decided to take up geology at the University of St Petersburg. He gave us a tour of his favourite sights in St Petersburg which included the rooftop of the University of St Petersburg. To get there we went up through a dingy looking attic which looked as if it was well used by students and up onto the roof, where there was a single, comfortable-looking armchair and wonderful views stretching out across the entire city. Just below us were the university gardens where Mikhail and his friends used to organise events and where they would also organise cleaning up parties afterwards so as to leave no mess. It felt very strange going home to Irina and her narrow set of rules.

I'm still not sure what made me stay with her for so long. I tried to move once but I came home to find her crying and suffering from a headache. One evening she asked me to come and watch television with her. 'Hannah darling! Come here please!' *'Hanochka idi siuda!'* She used this phrase often and it had exactly the same intonation every time. I remember wondering what opinion she had thought necessary to dispense for my welfare this time. But on this occasion she looked sad and vulnerable and just asked if I would watch television with her. She spread a cover over both of our legs and brought me some *kolbasa* (sausage). There was a series on Channel One called 'Despite everything I still love'. Over the course of my stay with her, we watched almost every episode together.

Hannah Collins was born in Norfolk in 1987. She studied Russian and French at the University of Nottingham and currently works as a translator.

A Cry from Solovki

John Butler's *pilgrimage to remote islands afforded him a rare view of Russia's soul. Sometimes, as he pondered the Communists' rage towards the clergy, the view was too much to bear*

In 863-869 AD Saint Cyril and Saint Methodius translated parts of the Bible into Old Church Slavonic for the first time, starting the growth of Christianity among the Slav peoples. There is evidence that the first Christian bishop was sent to Novgorod from Constantinople in around 866 AD. The Russian Orthodox Church today has about 150 million adherents worldwide. The Soviet regime was committed to the annihilation of religious institutions and ideas. During the first five years of Soviet power, the Bolsheviks executed 28 Russian Orthodox bishops and over 1,200 Russian Orthodox priests. Many others were imprisoned or exiled. In 1922, the Solovki Camp of Special Purpose, the first Russian concentration camp and a former Orthodox monastery, was established on the Solovki Islands in the White Sea. Eight metropolitans, twenty archbishops, and 47 bishops of the Orthodox Church died there, along with tens of thousands of the lay people.

AT the age of 47, my life as a farmer and married man fell to pieces. I entered several years of depression and aimless wandering from which I was fortunate to be accepted as a mature student at the Slavonic Studies department at Nottingham University in 1989. Five years later, too busy and interested to be depressed, I emerged with a degree. Now, with fresh reason to live, I gave myself to Russia. It wasn't difficult.

I'd never felt close to the world of man. I didn't know why, and the reproach of others that I should be more involved didn't help. Now, in Russia, for the first time in my life, I felt among my own people – who thought and felt as I did. I remember the pure joy of standing in queues at bus stops, sharing the cold and weariness, and feeling I belonged. I knew instinctively that everything I'd struggled with was known to them. And similarly, that all the heights and depths of their own lives was part of me. I couldn't not love them. I understood why I always seemed such a misfit at home. In at least half my nature, I was simply an exile from my own land.

As I search for my roots, I keep returning to Russia. It was amazing, but hardly surprising, to discover how much of her history, daily manners and religious expression is reflected in myself.

My mother, from Omsk in Siberia, was sent here to England at the age of nineteen, in 1923. She'd lost her family, lost just about everything – was cast adrift like millions of others in the chaos of revolution. In order to protect us, her children, from the traumas of her own experience, she rarely spoke about Russia, nor taught us the language, but subconsciously in character I took after her. When I stood for the first time on Russian soil, it all burst forth. After my first visit to Russia, in Spring 1991, I wrote:

> Russia is full of heart. I think that's why other people often find her hard to understand.

There's an oft quoted verse by Tiutchev that's worth remembering – translated, of course.

> *You cannot understand Russia with the intellect,*
> *Or measure her by ordinary standards.*
> *She has her own particular and special ways,*
> *In which you can only believe.*

The Russian heart easily overflows. It leads her people to excesses and extremes, yet endures and endures and endures. You don't see many old men in Moscow streets. Twenty million were killed in the last war alone and goodness only knows how many more were lost in 1914-18 and in the revolutionary wars and long, long years of purges and relocation. There's not a family in Russia that hasn't lost someone. You feel it still – everywhere. It grips your heart, it makes you cry. It's in their songs, it's in their lives and in the legions and legions of head-shawled old women who sweep the streets and stand in patient queues.

I stood before Lenin's tomb and yes, it's really there, and so are the gilded domes of the churches, and long-booted, fur-capped soldiers. Gradually I pieced together seventy years' abolishment of God, the substitution of Lenin for Christ, and a utopia in this world for the hope of a better one to come.

With the whole-hearted fervour so typically Russian, these people took everyone's dream of a more just and kindly world – and loved and forced and dragged it into existence. One stands absolutely amazed by what they've done. I know nothing, in scale, remotely comparable, though one remembers the gathering of our own strength that took place during the great wars. Russia sustained that fight when others ceased. She fought the Germans, her own poverty and backwardness, her fearsome climate, the wickedness and confusion within her own ideals, and the millions that protested and disagreed. Now the heroics are fraying at the edges.

One feels exhaustion. Western television undermines the belief that everything Soviet is best. The idol falls. That's what I found so heart-breakingly sad. That so much effort should ultimately fail. It's the lesson we all have to learn – that we are fallible, that life cannot be compelled and that most of us, sooner or later, find we need God. In the Kremlin gardens, beside a black marble statue of Lenin, stands a bowl of red roses; not far away, a constant flame burns on the tomb of the Unknown Soldier. In a children's playground, I found two tree-trunks carved into life-size figures of a mother beseeching her young soldier son. These things are Russian, straight from her heart, and you know they're eternal as Russia herself. *You cannot understand Russia with the intellect.*

Now, the restrictions are lifted and the churches are full of worshippers. Once more, tired bodies can gaze upon their dream. Bibles are sold in the streets and religious programmes appear on TV. These people loved their Tsar, they loved their revolution; they have to love something. Without it, they go flat. Their artistry, their creativity is emotional. But I wouldn't trust anyone who says it's 'this' or 'that'. The more I experience life, the less certain I am about anything and, for me, the Russian scene more than most others, defies analysis.

Readers who know about only half their family backgrounds will understand how important it was for me to find my Russian roots. At first, it was difficult to grasp the language, and find suitable accommodation. I also had to face the frightful consequences of Revolution and Civil War which had so deeply affected my mother, destroyed my family, and been passed to me. I soon realised that Russia's trials did not end there, nor those of her children, but continue for all of us, up to the present day. My mother died in 1992. Each day before the funeral, I sat with her in the morgue, feeling her spirit gradually withdraw. Then in Russia, I found her again: in countless ways, her Russian spirit showed. I remember wide-eyed little children, copies of herself, with songs and games; migrating birds flying south before the snow; warm Russian food. I watched with amazement as Russian women cut up vegetables and folded their linen, just as she had done. Of course – why not? – she was Russian, too. I followed the trail to Siberia where, one day, in a little chapel in Omsk, I remembered my 'lost' family and was quite sure they knew; were glad I'd come and that the spiritual contact was made.

In the early 1990s, following decades of isolation behind the Iron Curtain, few Russians had travelled abroad or even met a foreigner. I was a novelty, an object of interest – swept along on a wave of invitations to visit young and old and teach in different schools. Adults wanted to hear about the West and my Russian connections; children were avid for stories of my adventures around the world, encounters with animals and life as a farmer. Effortlessly, obviously, we had so much in common. I'd never taught in schools before, nor worked with children, but I soon learned. This brought me much happiness; it was so good to feel wanted. Between 1991 and 2005, I went to Russia sixteen times and stayed for more than five years in total. Mostly I lived in a small town about 100 kilometres south-west of Moscow, which became, and still is, my second home.

As my understanding of Russian improved, I started reading simple children's books introducing Orthodoxy and the Bible. I admired the gentle, but serious and uncompromising way in which they were presented. Gradually I advanced to the Gospels and daily prayers. I found this exercise of re-reading well-known themes in another language most helpful in bringing out fresh meaning I hadn't seen before. Similarly, attending Orthodox services brought me into a fresh appreciation of the Church.

The town, as with all post-revolutionary towns in Russia, was built without a church, and without any religious practice or education. The village church was ruined, desecrated, used as a stable, but enough was left to be repaired. Now it serves not only the few old parishioners who remember, but also the new, shy and unpractised from the town who are still discovering the lost traditions of their native faith.

In winter, we walk to the church through the snow, leaving behind our large, concrete blocks of flats to come to old houses built of logs and enclosing neat gardens behind wooden fences. Though here too, newly wealthy business people, seeking to escape the pressures of city life, are building modern homes. Showing from a distance above trees, the dome and belfry with their gilded crosses shine bright and new, but everything else about the church is poor. Few people have money to spare. Wealth belongs to 'new' Russia, not the old. You bow and cross yourself three times at the gate and then again at the door. A few beggars wait for alms. The inside is bare – no seats, a concrete floor, a few heating pipes and thick double windows to ward off the cold. There are high, grey walls beneath the dome and a few icons gathered from goodness knows where. This is no palace, no subsidised and artistic heritage; it's nothing but love rising from the ruins. They come to it and leave it in tears. Russia is full of tears.

It's normal to buy three candles: one for the dead, one for the living and one for the celebration of the day. Then, if the church is not too full, you go round and greet the icons. You get to know them, they become your friends, and you stand before them.

A Russian church is not designed for bodily comfort. 'Christ suffered,' they say, 'and so should we.' They take religion seriously. The two-hour evening service is considered necessary if you wish to receive the sacraments next morning, and you are expected to read the long preparatory prayers at home. Those ready to confess stand to the left and wait their turn. I was nervous at first. I had never confessed before and did not know what to do, or say. I watched the others but could not hear their words. The priest was kind but I felt I'd made a fool of myself. Only afterwards did I feel relief – that in spite of all my foolishness I was not rejected and that repentance is a process without end.

The congregation is mostly women, bundled in winter clothes – with thick felt boots and woollen shawls. Everyone knows it's the women who keep life going in Russia. You see their bent backs everywhere: bending to work or to carry or pray; tending to fields and streets and markets, their houses and children and the church. Often they've lost their men to war, to waste, to drink.

You can learn much about Russia by watching her old women – Mother Russia, Holy Beloved Mother. I watch them in church, feeling myself big and awkward but somehow, within myself, becoming as small as they. 'The sacrifices of God are a broken Spirit: A broken and a contrite heart, O God, thou wilt not despise.' So they read each morning in their prayers.

Before Liturgy at nine in the morning, there is half an hour of prayers, or a special remembrance for the dead. It is all done standing, close together, with an intensity of feeling that brings one easily to tears. 'Tears wash the soul,' they say. I've heard it described as 'throwing themselves at God'. But then, so much in Russia is extreme and feelings go from devotion to despair.

No family has escaped the terrible consequences of the Revolution. That awful guilt and suffering is there in all of us – it's everywhere. And when we remember the dead... O Lord, have mercy on us sinners.

All this is remembered each time I see one more new cupola or cross, or quiet women sitting in the marketplaces with stalls of holy icons and literature. There are Sunday schools now for both children and adults, and religious programmes on radio and television. Churches are usually well attended. Indeed, on festive days you may not be able to get in for the crowd. You can speak without fear; and those churches lucky enough to have a bell can ring. That's enough for now – that in Russia today, for all her sins, we hear her bells again. And in our little town, plans have been formed to build a new church in the main square next to the music school and library and across the road from the department store. I think nearly everyone is glad.

I felt great love for this little church and its people, who seemed so like my own kin, and I wanted to participate in the worship. It was a happy day when, in 1997, just before my sixtieth birthday, I was formally included. No doubt this helped my prayers, but more noticeable was the way in which life now branched out into even more varied human connections. With the many friendships I'd made through teaching, I found myself on a tide of love and being loved as I had never known before.

In August 2004, we set out by bus from St Petersburg for a long, long journey north to see how Orthodoxy had returned to Solovki.

Pilgrimage is a common feature of Russian religious life. Because of the distance between places and general lack of facilities, many churches and monasteries expect to receive and provide for groups of visitors. More formal, organised tours by bus and train operate at minimal expense and comfort, but Russians are stoical in hardship and expect pilgrimage to include a measure of self-sacrifice.

Typically rather rushed affairs with much travelling, brief visits and loquacious guides, you get taken to places you would never otherwise see, and build up an historical and contemporary picture of the faith. I cannot speak for their spiritual content which depends, of course, on the pilgrims and how they react to what's provided. 'Be it unto you according to your faith.' Most visits are connected with saints. Russia has many and Orthodoxy makes the most of them. It's always inspiring to see where and how they lived and to learn about their lives. There's usually ample opportunity to venerate the customary holy objects, and partake of holy springs. In addition, for me, pilgrimage provides precious views of more ordinary Russian life and landscape. No-one can really know Russia until silenced and humbled by her forests, exalted by her space. Russia is so much more than man.

Since repression was relaxed, there's been a quite extraordinary resurrection of faith, with the rebuilding of ruined churches and restoration of religious life. However, after three generations of lost practice such fresh enthusiasm can hardly be mature. Priests tend to be young and inexperienced; churches rebuilt according to tradition cannot be holier than they are; and the many elaborate rituals of Orthodoxy easily get taken for the truth they serve.

It is not unusual for those people who seek a deeper communion with God to distance themselves from their fellows to pray, silent and alone. Who knows how many live and die that way? But some attract a few followers who, of necessity, develop some organisation. This process is well recognised in Orthodoxy and certainly most Russian monasteries started this way. It is worth remembering that the communal living and elaborate church services familiar to pilgrims are often the very conditions the founder figures sought to avoid.

Russia's northern forests are indescribably beautiful when seen from a bus window, but surprisingly hostile once you step outside. Undergrowth is often impenetrable, marsh impassable, and countless insects eat you alive. It's easy to see why early travellers preferred to float past on the many connecting rivers and lakes. Thus it was that, in 1429, monks from Belozersk came to Solovki – a group of small islands in the White Sea, not far south of the Arctic Circle. What started as a simple hermitage developed into the greatest monastic fortress and administrative centre of Northwest Russia. However, following the Revolution of 1917 it was taken over by the Communists. It became the first of many Gulag slave labour camps, and a place for the extermination of priests. About a million prisoners were sent here to work and die. Many haunting reminders of those dreadful days remain – of plagues and executions, of mass graves, of every kind of horror inflictable by man on man, of desolation and distance from civilised life, and of passed souls known but to God. Now, again, monastic life is reappearing. One church functions and many pilgrims come during the short summer, but conditions for them remain primitive and the overall atmosphere is grim.

Having to face the facts of those men and women, starved, frozen, worked and tormented to death is a huge exercise in faith. In Spirit no-one dies, we know – in God, all live. But, Oh my God – my ears still echo with the groans; imagination sees, my heart still cries. Throughout all Russia, there's hardly a family not affected.

But time has passed and life goes on. Whatever was it all? Some nightmare dream? One is forced to search again and again for what is real. Following Lenin's instruction to 'shoot as many of the clergy as possible', some 200,000 priests, monks and nuns were killed. All monasteries and 99 per cent of churches were desecrated, ransacked or destroyed. Why did it happen? Some years ago, when Patriarch Alexii II was asked this question, he replied: 'To cure us of a monstrous pride.' It's an answer to remember. I don't suppose he referred only to the Church, but that's where my mind became focused while on Solovki. Why was the Church so hated? What aroused such anger in the people? Forgive me if I offend, but I feel compelled to look for reasons. They are etched with blood into the stones of Solovki – they are part of one's experience there and lessons for us to learn.

What causes us so to rise up against our brethren? The question is as old as history and it seems a part of pilgrimage that we all have to undertake. The sins of the Church are nothing new – they were clearly described by Jesus, and are no different today. The monster pride is always there, lurking behind the show. It's easy to see the sins of others, but what about our own? What is the basic pride? Is it not that we think and believe we have an existence separate and apart from God – an ego, which manifests itself as 'my' mind and body, an imaginary creature of time and space; limited, corruptible, mortal and, above all, concerned for its own survival? A monstrous pride indeed, and don't we hang on to it! Call it sin, pride, ignorance or folly – the basic human error is that I am mortal, separate mind and body, and not the spiritual image of God. And so long as we believe this, so we will have monstrous, distorted ego minds to plan every device of evil, and monstrous bodies to play them out – get diseased, tormented, and to die.

Do I need to list what happens, to both Church and ourselves? I think not, for this is exactly what the ego loves – criticism of others, justification of itself and belief in its reality. It doesn't help Spirit to dwell upon the flesh but how do we get out of it? Like a universal hypnosis or dream, it holds us captive. Yes, us. As much as those captives of the Gulag sat inside their dungeons, so are we captives of belief in our mortality.

Solovki is a place where whatever spiritual understanding one has is put to the test. The dream, if it is a dream, is only too horribly real. On one occasion, the unearthly clarity of northern skies, unfolding dramatically above us like improbable illustrations in exotic travel brochures, reminded me how, in Revelation, life itself is described as a book (Rev. 20: 12). As pages are turned, we see Russia, England, pictures of Gulags, icons of heaven, our own lives and our deeds both good and bad. What happens to them when the page is turned? And what are we? The reader/witness – or the one described?

All these events in our memories and imagination are terribly real and important so long as we believe and hang on to them, but times come when we stand back, let go, and realise that all that mental burden has dissolved away – just as a dream, when we wake up. Then, questions of religion dissolve away with everything else. Meanwhile, the world rolls on, and within its ever changing scenes, individual souls continue to live out their own personal dreams. Eventually, it is said, every creature wakes up, or comes to salvation – but that's another story. I can only tell you mine, and how I coped with my pilgrimage to Solovki.

The pilgrims celebrated the 'Triumph of Orthodoxy' but I could not join in – not in the seen and spoken sense. To me, the victory seemed incomplete. The old, red star of Communism lay bent and rusty in the Solovki museum. Cross goes up, star comes down, and I felt the ancient boulders of which the church is built heave a patient sigh. They've seen it all before. One lot of men, one temple, or one set of words replace another. I recall an event in church early one morning when monks lined up with their backs to us. Hidden behind their long, black hats and cloaks, nothing human was visible at all. No more man – just silence. In that moment, for the first time in Solovki church, I felt unthreatened. God save us from ourselves. All things temporal and tangible need to be laid aside and transcended if we really want to be free. Church traditions, yes, and priests themselves which inspire to start our journey, can become psychological barriers in our progress to spiritual maturity. Though, God knows, it can be worse without them. Although each liturgy warns us against putting our trust in 'Princes, or any child of man' (Ps. 146: 3), we do so again and again – and who is to blame if the priestly ego swells?

I found the Church on Solovki unsympathetic. As I stood listening to the never-ending words, I felt, God forgive me, history repeating itself. Did not similar dogmatic voices lecture similarly leg-weary prisoners standing in the yard outside? And are not similar queues which then waited fearfully lest they were refused their earthly bread, now waiting at confession for priestly sanction (a Russian requirement) to eat the bread of God? At times I could take no more and had to go out where the quieter assurances of grass and sky took me beyond the sullied world of man.

Deception, however, did its work in me. Both then and afterwards I fell into criticism; seeing sinister parallels between persecutor and persecuted in dress, screens, images, authority; confessions in the name of Christ, or anti-Christ; threats of retribution; conform – or else, and 'them and us'. There's nothing one ego loves or hates more than another one, and in this sewer of conflict I was too engulfed to see any better.

As history shows, Church Militant is only too capable of being its own monster of pride and persecution. The true Church is not a creature of earthly material and human speech at all. It's no more its earthly body and thoughts than I am mine. As explained (Matt. 16: 15-19), its foundation is recognition of the 'I am, Thou art' of man. In our quest for identity, forgetful of our spiritual selves, we so easily lurch from one system to another – from politics to religion, and lose our simple being, in between. Forgive me if I offend. I know there's a time and a place for all these different things. I never cease to be grateful for my own early schooling in the faith, but now I am old and have less need of show. The words, the practices that led me onwards then, are now behind. Now, like the early pioneers of Solovki, I choose silence and solitude for prayer.

But, finding such contrasts there, within myself – how could they be contained? Such beauty of nature, such sorrow of man; such titanic proportions of the struggle between good and evil; such love and hatred of the Church. There's no escaping the fact of one's own responsibility. The more we open ourselves to union, the more we bear the sins of others too. It's no use blaming 'them', for they are 'me'. There can be few places on earth where the darkness of man and the goodness of God are so starkly presented. The pilgrimage organisers warned us how it would be – how easily we might find ourselves angered, arguing, depressed. Certainly I have seldom, if ever, felt these polarities of man and God so agonisingly opposed, yet both within me, tearing my being apart. Dare I say that in those tortured hours, I felt closer to Jesus on the cross, and, looking to Him, knew He also knew.

A few hours across the sea from Solovki, there's a neighbouring island called Anzer, which was also part of the Gulag. Here, in 1712, appearing in a vision, the Holy Mother told St Job to name a certain hill Golgotha and build there a Church of the Crucifixion. It was later discovered that this is on exactly the same longitude as Golgotha, Jerusalem. Consistent with its name, and as part of the policy of profanation, the church building itself was used for the imprisonment and martyrdom of priests. How many died there, no-one knows, but even today, on this hallowed place, a self-sown birch tree grows in the shape of a cross. In the heightened atmosphere of pilgrimage, such miraculous happenings seem quite normal.

There were saints also on Solovki and their tombs are in the church, but I found the place so smothered in the struggles and agonies of man that I never really got through to them. However, as we returned from Anzer, on a magical evening of clear, northern light, we saw some whales. It was most noticeable how the whole company of watching pilgrims burst into spontaneous joy. It seemed that by then, we'd all had enough of both the wickedness and righteousness of man, and were only too ready to throw off that oppression and respond to the glories of natural Grace. Watching the pristine beauty of the White Sea – the harmony of water, cloud and sky, I was reminded of angelic singing, with one heart, one voice. This now included us, renewed, awoken – we ourselves, as children freed from monstrous dreams, no more bewailing the forgotten past but rejoicing in creation as it really is. Who could not love the whales, the seals and birds – the lovely, lovely sea? Even as I write, I cry – that such extremes are in the heart of man. And thinking of that time, I'm quite sure I was closer then to the spirit of Solovki's saints than when I was trying to do what I thought was expected of me before their tombs in church.

During the long return journey, we passed through Kondopoga, and found there an ancient wooden church, with a sweet, simple icon of the Dormition, and a little, old lady caretaker. With thoughtful, unobtrusive service, she opened the shutters to let in the light and did all that was necessary. After the struggles of Solovki, all was quiet, unpretentious, gentle – warm, pure and natural as wood itself. I was reminded that faith, in its maturity is always kind, modest, and 'Seeketh not her own' (1 Cor. 13:5). There's something about wooden houses and churches especially dear to a Russian soul, and it's not hard to understand why. Even the Communists had not destroyed this one. Instinctively, I stroked the hewn, log walls. Here, there were no priests; modest icons and church equipment were hardly noticeable in the dim light; no voices broke the peace; nothing was demanded or thrust upon us. It's so much easier to love humility. After the forces of Solovki, the relief was immense. Here was faith in the mature sweetness of simple knowing, with no need to assert it. Here was a Church where I could give my heart – and it brought me to tears.

And then, after Kondopoga, we came to the monastery of St Alexander Svirsky, well-known for the fact that his body has remained undecayed since his death in 1533. It was impressive to see but, for me at least, not what really mattered. While pilgrims prostrated themselves and read their prayers, a conscious presence filled the space – both with us and watching us. He was, he is. And outside too, he is. He was, as us, a body of earth; he is present, timelessly present, but completely awake, free, and beyond creation's dream. What are 500 years to a fully wakened soul? And being near his awakeness, even to us in earth, the grass seemed greener, flowers brighter, a little bird crossing the path more perfect than before. Is this not sanctity, and demonstration of eternal life? What are we doing if we honour a shrivelled, dark thing in a box and ignore the glorious freedom beaming all around us?

This was Church transcendent and forever; another world from the battles of Solovki, where men argue and fight and ever will do. This needs no walls, or words of man. Here, beyond time and space, there's no more need of bodies, decayed or undecayed, for consciousness is free. Both Gulag and Church on Earth lose their significance and fade, for they existed only in the human mind. The strife is finished and the work is done; the dream is over, and we come to rest.

Postscript

This article was not one of those that flowed by itself. I found it extraordinarily difficult to write; struggle, struggle all the way – at least at the beginning – exactly as we struggle with evil. I was trying to discuss causes and effects – as if I knew – and getting mixed up with my own prejudices. And then I realised that discussing the dualities of the world is always confusing, because the basic subject-matter is unreal. Even if we only half believe in them, we try to make sense of a world of shadows. Back home in England, and once more on the Derbyshire hills, we sat, one sunny afternoon in peace. I remembered Jesus' last words of peace – 'Peace I leave with you' (John 14: 27). Deeper and deeper I felt the peace, the endless peace. Nothing, but nothing could be not at peace, but only the wilfulness of restless mind.

John Butler describes himself as a farmer, teacher, traveller and writer. At a low ebb, in the Arizona desert, he met Jesus, a turning point in his life, shifting the focus of his spiritual practice from meditation to prayer. In the late 1980s he returned to university in England to study Russian so that he could visit his mother's homeland, which he first did in 1991. This led to a period of teaching in Russia, where he learnt more about the Orthodox practice of 'prayer of the heart'.

Excess and Contradiction in Russia

*A chance trip to Russia to play mini-rugby led **Daniel Kearvell** into a decade of immersion in post-Soviet culture. Breakfast with cognac over business meetings in Archangelsk became the norm. But despite marrying a Russian, he accepts he will always be seen as an outsider*

Nashi is a political youth movement in Russia which declares itself to be a democratic, anti-fascist, anti-oligarchic-capitalist movement. Its creation was encouraged by senior figures in the Russian administration and, by late 2007, it had grown in size to about 120,000 members, aged mainly between 17 and 25. According to its leader, Vasily Yakemenko, Nashi in 2010 alone received funding of about 200 million roubles from the Russian state budget.

Introduction

IT WAS fate that decreed that Russia would always be a part of my life. At least, if I were Russian, I think that this is what I should say. Fatalism is not a traditional reference point in an Englishman's philosophical armoury, although I often wonder just how different things would have been had one of my father's friends not written that drunken letter to Denis Thatcher in 1989. The surprise reply from the husband of the Prime Minister set in motion a series of events which led to my local mini rugby side being the first junior club to host a team from the Soviet Union that year, and subsequently to travel to play rugby in Moscow, St Petersburg and Kazakhstan during the early 1990s. Without stretching the point, and certainly with a nod to the fanciful, I might claim that while I didn't choose Russia, perhaps Russia chose me. The school project on Russia was followed by a degree in Russian, the best part of ten years in the country, a Russian wife and even a stint on Russian TV commentating on the 2003 Rugby World Cup. As I write, it is a source of great pride that two of the boys we first encountered 21 years ago in Zelenograd, Moscow, in 1990, have just made their Rugby World Cup debuts as part of the Russian team making its first ever appearance in the tournament.

Throughout my association with Russia, a constant feature of my relationship with the country is how noticeably I have been unable to shake off its almost magnetic attraction. To this day Russia seems to exert a force upon me which is incessant and unyielding. It is a sense, a state of mind even, that was first conveyed to me by my school teacher of Russian – that you can leave Russia, but it'll never leave you. A university lecturer put it in rather more alarming terms – that it's a drug that you'll never be able to rid yourself of.

Student Life

Russia can be quite a dangerous place sometimes, but I never think about it.

Marc Almond

It is said that life as a student ought to provide worthwhile academic experiences and represent solid preparation for the challenges of later life. Indeed, one university describes a Year Abroad in Russia as being seen by employers as 'proof of adaptability, independence and resourcefulness'. Certainly, as an employer in Russia, I saw it as an opportunity to ascertain the levels of curiosity the young undergraduate had shown during his or her time in the motherland. It is probably no exaggeration to say that my own Year Abroad in Russia was high on life experience, if a little more moderate on academic progression. The year we spent in Russia was simply one of the most exhilarating of my life, the legacy of which was both lasting and ultimately life-changing. It has been said that time in Russia as an undergraduate defines your future relationship with the country. The country was not, and is not, to everybody's taste, to which the numbers of those departing courses ahead of schedule testified. One's interest in Russia either became a lifelong passion or a temporary educational assignment to be undertaken until heading for more mainstream pursuits. For many of us, it was simply the time of our lives.

Voronezh

Well: live long, black earth: be firm, clear-eyed – here there's a black-voiced silence working

Osip Mandelstam

Voronezh, the capital of Russian Black Earth territory, and the venue for our eighteen-week Year Abroad course, was a raw, gritty city at the turn of the century. Our group consisted of twenty students from different British universities and we lived with local families. My arrival caused my family to sleep four to a room to ensure that I was provided with my own bedroom. Voronezh represented the opportunity to immerse ourselves in four months of relative freedom, fun and independence – and vodka, which was dangerously available at that time for around 10p a shot. It was always going to be an explosive combination. At that price it was easy to comprehend how the average Russian male consumed over 90 litres of vodka a year and why Russian consumption of hard liquor accounted for some 50 percent of the world's total. The familiar comments about Russians only feeling comfortable with acquaintances they had got drunk with turned out to be one of the few truisms among the popular Russian myths and stereotypes. It is true that during our time in the city our group made more than a few lifelong friends.

Soon after arriving, some of our group were to learn that explosive was indeed an all-too literally apt description of Voronezh at that time, as a grenade was thrown at the building they were living in. One of our friends was even involved in an international spying scandal, and was sentenced to three years in prison, of which he subsequently served six months. We ended up unwelcome guests at several local establishments, partly on account of the group's collective liking for the local alcoholic delights, and our corresponding inability to handle them. However, for all the scrapes with the local constabulary, threats of extortion from our 23-stone gym instructor and various threats from student body representatives in Moscow, somehow, we all survived the experience. From walking in the Caucasus, to hitching on a horse and cart in Belarus, to spontaneously teaching English in Nizhny Novgorod schools; the experience, both in Voronezh and during the extensive travel around Russia we embarked upon during the holidays, was simply life-changing. The warmth with which we were welcomed is my overwhelming recollection of Voronezh. Returning recently, ten years to the month later, we found that little had changed; hospitality on a grand scale was accorded, and it was heartening to see that the city – aesthetically at least – had benefitted from some welcome investment in its façades. However, the familiar daily issues of unpaid wages still dogged the families we had lived with. It was a time that defined the group, as individuals, as friends, and many of our futures, cementing what for me was to become a lifelong relationship with Russia. Voronezh, one of the least glamorous and yet most lastingly evocative of places, had confirmed what I had previously suspected; that I had to get back out to Russia, on a full-time basis, as soon as possible.

Career

I do not rule Russia; ten thousand clerks do
Nicholas I

Outside the teaching profession, opportunities to relocate as a professional to the country immediately after graduation were few and far between, and the route back via the corporate ladder was likely to be lengthy and without guarantee of that elusive Russian posting.

In my penultimate year at university, I was fortunate to have the opportunity to work as an intern for the Russo-British Chamber of Commerce (RBCC). As an NGO, and trade facilitator, it was the ideal starting point to become acquainted with the Russo-British business environment and, as with many NGOs, it offered the opportunity to be entrusted with tasks and projects of real value. One such project was compiling a business plan to open an office for the Chamber in St Petersburg. Having spent the second part of my year abroad teaching English in St Petersburg schools, I had fallen in love with the city and was desperate to return. I eagerly volunteered, at my own cost and while studying for my final year exams, to travel to the city on a number of occasions to research and lobby for opening an office in the city. My optimism that the city's cultural magnificence simply had to correspond to a wealth of opportunities for RBCC – a hunch which was later proved to be right, if not quite for the same naïve logic as presented in my initial business case – was not shared by the RBCC Executive Committee, who in 2001 rejected my proposal. My disappointment at having spent much of my final year engaged in this failed project was tempered somewhat by the offer of a job in the RBCC Moscow office. It was an offer I eagerly accepted, and would not live to regret.

I was on the princely wage of £800 per month and Moscow was a whirlwind of meetings and mischief. My first three months passed in a blur. History will no doubt recall the mid to late 1990s as being the time of extremes – the Wild East, as Russia was dubbed at the time – but my roommate and I, two young professional (in name at least) Englishmen, left no stone unturned in search of what might be termed adventure and challenge. In between the haze, I managed to achieve some success in my commercial role for RBCC, and after two happy years in Moscow, was finally given the opportunity to prove once and for all that my St Petersburg proposal was commercially viable. In 2004, I moved up to the Northern Capital to be the Director of RBCC St Petersburg, from where after three years I was given the opportunity to become General Manager for a large multi-national company, with responsibility for the West Region of Russia. Working both in non-commercial and commercial environments was a fascinating experience, particularly when acting as a consultant to UK companies during my RBCC days. As one of my Russian friends from an RBCC member company once told me: 'When I opened a business, the question wasn't if we'd be successful, but whether we'd be able to keep it.' Having said that, the opportunities for the culturally and commercially astute remain significant, and it is a matter of huge personal pride that RBCC continues to thrive in the city to this day.

Clearly, life and work in the Northern Capital was not without its challenges, and I am not just talking about being forced to wash down my breakfast with cognac over business meetings in Archangelsk, having my wife approached by the security services, or braving a propeller-driven plane from Murmansk to Archangelsk, a journey so terrifying that at least half the plane disembarked utterly legless. The sheer geographical expanse of Northwest Russia – twice the size of Europe – presented its own challenges, and I fondly remember the stoicism of the driver in our company who was responsible for the St Petersburg-Murmansk delivery leg – a mere 28-hour journey, borne without a hint of complaint. My responsibilities spanned the Arctic Circle and beyond, looking after the most northerly office in the world for my company. In true Russian style, though, where there is hardship, there is hospitality. Despite being urged to join the *morzhi* (walruses), the name for people fond of swimming in holes in the ice during the Festival of the North, an experience which even now makes me shiver, it was the warm welcome of the regions that is my abiding memory.

Living with and observing fellow foreigners in Russia, it seemed to me that the majority chose to live outside of local communities in what Andrew Meier (author of *Black Earth*) describes as 'Western ghettos'. Some, typically long-term expats, mostly with Russian spouses, immerse themselves in Russian-speaking professional and social environments, planning their holidays around the time the hot water is turned off, feeling guilty about whistling indoors and reeling away in horror if someone tries to shake their hand over the threshold of a doorway (all of which I have been guilty of at one stage or another). In truth I spent much of the ten years I lived in the country sub-consciously oscillating between the two, finding company in purely Russian environments, but also in the familiar foreign communities and activities of the capital cities. Upon discovering that St Petersburg had no rugby club, for instance, I felt compelled to establish one. Despite becoming close to Russian culture and lifestyle, over time, paradoxically, I became aware of the increasingly strong draw of my own values, background and upbringing.

My time in Russia proved that for all the riddles, mysteries and enigmas that are part of the fabric of Russian society, it is the country's sense of fun that is surely unrivalled. It explains why so many long-term expats leave Russia only to return a year or so later.

Nash, nasha, nashe, nashi

From the time of Richard Chancellor, the first British explorer to land upon Russian shores in 1553 (albeit lost, on the way to China), to modern-day Western veterans of Russia, the country's allure remains heady and irresistible. Chancellor, himself by no means the last lost foreign soul to stumble across Russia, earned himself an audience with Tsar Ivan IV (the Terrible), an encounter which eventually led to the foundation of the Muscovy trading company and birth of formal Russo-British commercial relations. Despite my many years in Russia, I never lost sight of the country's exoticism and extent of her *difference* – to me one of the most striking aspects of Russian society. However European the country's veneer may seem, however increasingly cosmopolitan the citizens of the country's capital are becoming, there is never any doubt in Russia that you are *foreign* and in an alien land. Literally, as the Russian has it, you are a foreign (*ino*) alien, or wanderer (*stranets*).

Your appearance still marks you out, even in the second decade of the twenty-first century. When you step on to any public transport you are subject to the scrutiny of your fellow travellers. When you walk down the street in any Russian town, you will be stared at. Ten years ago, despite your best attempts, in no way could you hide the fact that you were not '*nash*' (ours, or one of us), but an *inostranets*, a foreigner. These days you, the *inostranets*, are a little less immediately obvious, perhaps more as a consequence of the globalisation of fashion, rather than any significant increase in multiculturalism in Russian society. You are undeniably less of a novelty, with significantly less curiosity value than a decade ago – due to both the steady trickle of foreigners visiting Russia for business or tourism, and to the explosion of outbound foreign tourism that has given Russians the opportunity to explore the globe

My first impressions of Russia were that many of the formal demarcations of 'Us' and 'Them' within society remain firmly in place. The theatres and museums had a two-tier pricing policy, in which the foreigner would pay twice as much for his cinema ticket as the Russian. Hotels, particularly the less salubrious, would often refuse to take Westerners. I recall one particularly less-than-happy 4am morning as a student, touring Minsk hotels for three hours attempting to find an establishment that was prepared to go to the trouble of registering our documents. Even latterly, we were turned away by one regional Russian hotel simply because the establishment was not prepared to register foreigners. It amuses me to think back to those immediate post-Communist days, as I did recently when one of my friends got turned away at an upmarket Moscow establishment, just because '*Eto Moskva*' (This is Moscow), the implication being that my friend was neither Russian, nor up to the particular standards demanded of those deemed worthy of entering the place.

It worked in reverse too: when I first arrived in Moscow in 1990, as part of the first British rugby team to play in the country, we were amazed to see the orderly three-hour queue for the newly-opened McDonalds on Pushkin Square. We, as foreigners, were allowed straight in and were pushed straight to the front of the queue by our Russian hosts. No-one complained. The same scenario repeated itself at Gorky Park.

Russia's 'difference' is not today as striking to the first-time visitor for the reasons I have mentioned. But the sense of difference is being expressed in other ways, such as the mushrooming of social-awareness campaigns on billboards proclaiming: 'My Russia, My Family', or 'Build a Stronger Russia', or 'Russia – together we are stronger'. In recent times, these Soviet-style campaigns, with their Soviet-style slogans, have become more and more widespread, to the extent that such socially-driven billboards now account for over a quarter of the total of all the city's street advertising.

The word which continues to fascinate, and which for me sums up much of this movement, is *'nash'* in all its forms – masculine, feminine, neuter and plural. Just what, or who, was meant by this word 'ours' that my friends and colleagues kept mentioning? Why was *Nashi* chosen by Putin as the name of the Youth Movement of United Russia in 2006? How did this sit with the fact that for years the Soviet population had been told that their homeland was not Russia but the USSR? (*'Nasha rodina – SSSR.'*) And frankly, don't our Western sensibilities counsel that such an overt delineation of foreigner and non-foreigner is now taboo?

Nash, it seemed to me, tacitly accepts the fact that Russians are different, perhaps even superior, to outsiders, both in the literal political meaning and the metaphorical, more intangible mystical manner. This idea is not a new one. The idea of the superiority of the Russian national character has its roots in the Orthodoxy of pre-Soviet times, and socialism during the Soviet Union. Linked to this has been the constant existence of threat from outside parties and doctrines, of the common enemy, spoken or unspoken, be it the opposing pillars of Christianity and Islam or the capitalist ideologies and external threat posed by the West and United States in particular. Yet the demise of socialism and the damage done during the Soviet period to the previously unquestioned belief in the Orthodox faith has shaken these previously irrefutable foundations of what is 'ours'. In recent times, particularly in the twenty-first century, policy seems to have been directed into creating a myriad of 'outside' parties seemingly intent on undermining and/or destroying Russia. Since the fall of the USSR, Russia has variously positioned itself both as an ally of or in opposition to the West, without cementing its position in either camp. Open conflict with Georgia, the gas crises with the Ukraine and Russia's positioning over the West's involvement in Libya and on the issue of sanctions against Syria are recent examples of open differences and conflict with the wider international community. Russia under Putin has sought a place at the centre of international affairs, as an equal, and as a country that is prepared to go counter to international opinion if in its own national interest.

Domestically, the government's increasing authoritarianism and gradual dismantling of the constitution has already required compelling ideological foundations and the perceived existence of threat, real or otherwise, on the pretext of averting social disorder. After the Beslan tragedy, elections for regional governors were cancelled; one of the clearest examples of such an approach. My own experiences suggest that mistrust of outsiders is still fairly widespread in Russia. In a country where it is reckoned that there are still over a million people involved in security activities, perhaps this is not surprising. I heard 'Yankee go home' more than a few times, and was interrogated and presumed to be engaged in surreptitious activities on behalf of my homeland in Ekaterinburg, after I had made the rather foolish mistake of travelling to the city while my visa was being renewed. The British Council, which at its peak boasted fourteen representative offices and one and a half million users across Russia, was closed down in the regions over a tax dispute. The affair, which had flared up at a difficult time for Russo-British relations, in the midst of disagreements over espionage and the Litvinenko affair, was huge international news. As both sides claimed provocation, the Russians' approach demonstrated that there was only going to be one winner. In no uncertain terms, at the dead of night, visits to the homes of local British Council employees made it clear that they were not to appear for work the next day. Political hardball on their home turf is a game which the Russians seldom lose.

The contradiction of warmth and fear is widespread. How is it that, despite being proud to the point of nationalism, so many Russians, when travelling abroad, go out of their way to avoid meeting Russians or, in extreme cases, even speaking Russian? How can pride and shame in one's country be such evident bedfellows? Indeed, how can a country so collectively proud treat their fellow Russian comrades, particularly strangers, with what can only be described as contempt?

Suffering and Pride

The most basic, most rudimentary spiritual need of the Russian people is the need for suffering, ever-present and unquenchable, everywhere and in everything
Fyodor Dostoevsky

The contradictions seem to begin in the Russian psyche. Despite keeping the world, politically at least, at arms-length, it is rare to find a more openly hospitable people than the Russians. But dig beneath the surface and you uncover what to the outsider appears to be startling melancholy. Given the extent of the country's suffering, this is of course not surprising. The development of civil society, following a century in which it is estimated some 50 million people died as a result of wars or repression, was very much of secondary consideration.

The First World War saw Russia lose nearly two million men, while by conservative estimates five million died during the ensuing Civil War and over a million more during the Great Terror of 1937-38. During the Second World War – or the Great Patriotic War as it is known in Russia – of 1941-45, it is estimated that every third family lost a member. During the horror of the siege of Leningrad, cannibalism was allegedly rife as the Germans laid siege to the city for 900 days, resulting in 1.5 million casualties. During the Battle of Stalingrad, every other citizen of the city died. Russia was by no means alone in having suffered during the world wars, yet this, when taken into consideration alongside the emigration of much of the country's intellectual elite during the 1970s and 1980s, the collapse of the Soviet Union in 1991 and the financial crisis of 1998 – which saw families' life-savings wiped out in a day as the rouble was devalued – it is some roll-call of suffering. As Meier notes: 'Suffering had become the national occupation'.

Following difficult and tragic periods in their respective nations' histories, it is revealing to compare the reaction of post-Soviet Russian society with that of post-Nazi Germany. The generations of Germans after the Second World War produced a fresh wave of both reflection on and re-birth from the Nazi period, in a kind of national penitence. To the Russians, the idea of national contrition for the horrors of the past was simply not palatable, despite Boris Yeltsin's sporadic attempts in the mid-1990s to build national conscience upon something other than mass slogan and campaigns. The failure of this has been a major contributor towards the increasing 'creation of enemies' syndrome witnessed throughout the Putin era.

Personally, I always felt that the past was too painful a topic ever to visit in any depth with my Russian friends and acquaintances. Undeniably, the past has created the pre-conditions for the development of the present form of Russian society. It is a society in which those who lived through misery have no desire for reflection upon memories, which still seem too raw. For those too young to remember Soviet times, the past simply does not seem of relevance. Perhaps tellingly, the word 'catharsis' has not entered general usage in Russian and is used only in specialist contexts. Following a century that witnessed the destruction and departure of so many of the country's intellectual and political elite, it is hardly surprising that the gene pool, too, has suffered.

Putin, a man of the Soviet system, has frequently displayed a conciliatory and even warm attitude towards the country's past. This approach is likely to be – at least in part – a result of genuine pride in the system in which he grew up. Politically too, such sentiments are expedient, given the significant support still enjoyed by those who would seek a return to the stabilities of the socialist past. To this day, a large percentage of the older generation recalls the Soviet period as a time when living standards were higher. According to official statistics, they were. Official poverty levels in the late Soviet period were as low as 1.5%, a fraction of today's figure. The gradual rehabilitation of the Soviet past, including a reappraisal and softening of Stalin's image, in school textbooks in recent years has been a reflection of Putin's policy of re-introducing national pride, as well as a re-positioning of Russia's dealings in the foreign policy.

At home, Russians continue to revere the Soviet Union's military achievements, particularly those of the Great Patriotic War. Russians, justifiably, consider that it was they who had rescued the world from German occupation, and are acutely aware of the devastation the country suffered in the process. In St Petersburg, one of Nevsky Prospect's most vivid inscriptions reads: 'During bombardment, this side of the street is more dangerous.' Although there is a political reticence to commemorate victims of Stalin's Great Terror in 1937-38, during which the purge of the officer class significantly weakened the subsequent war effort, Victory Day is celebrated with a public holiday and parades across the country. Car stickers proclaiming *'Spasibo dedu, za pobedu!'* (Thanks for the victory, Grandad!) are familiar sights in today's Russia.

National Conscience

The Russian people are the only source of power
V. V. Putin

The people are silent
Pushkin, Boris Godunov, at the Tsar's inauguration

During my initial teenage acquaintance with Russian culture I read and re-read George Orwell's classic *Nineteen Eighty-Four*. I was fascinated by the dystopian society portrayed in the book, and drew constant parallels between Winston Smith's tragic predicament and the fate of some of the people I had met in Russia. After the Soviet Union fell, it left behind questions and gaps where previously there had been certainty, identity, and ideals, courtesy of the all-encompassing Soviet Big Brother. What was national conscience in the new Russia? Was it Soviet, Russian, socialist, nationalist or Orthodox? Ethnicity became a major issue for debate within Russia's many diverse ethnic groups, some of which made unsuccessful breakaway attempts. Many Russians, in fact, seemed to consider that their spirituality was closest to Russian literature and culture, the one aspect of national identity that was almost universally a constant and dependable source of pride and pleasure for the Russian people. As the famous phrase goes, Pushkin was, and remained, for Russians '*nashe vse*' – 'our everything'.

A comparison of Russia's national identity struggle with that of other nations reveals that, of the European nations that have wielded power and influence, the majority have their own versions of the 'supreme': a sense that their doctrines, religions and beliefs ought to be spread throughout their empires and to the wider world. Anthony Smith, a pre-eminent theorist on national identity, considers that an understanding of missionary nationalism assists in gaining an insight into the Russian national consciousness. Within this, he argues, there are four criteria: moral superiority, reversal of lowly status, strict outsiders' boundary and mobilisation of the people as a whole. He claims that Russians on the whole do not associate their identity with physical boundaries, but more with spiritual and cultural concepts and ideas. The idea in itself is interesting, as recent conflicts with both the Ukraine and Georgia demonstrate the extent to which Russia is willing to go to maintain – if not extend – her sphere of influence. Alexander Solzhenitsyn, meanwhile, argued that missionary Soviet idealism was an artificial ideal taken from Western countries, and that such a single, universal ideology could not serve as a binding and developing force for the country's future and sense of national conscience.

Westerners and Slavophiles have historically held opposing views as to the direction the country ought to take. The fall of Communism again brought this debate into sharp focus, even if it seemed clear that, as Anatoly Chubais, a key Yeltsin adviser, put it: 'I don't think Russia will follow the United States way. I don't think Russia will follow the French way. I'm sure Russia will find its own way'. Frequently in Russia one hears that democracy is not suitable for Russia. Without doubt, the experience of the 1990s thoroughly discredited Western-style democracy in Russia. Russians resented the presence of Western advisors, associating capitalism with the bandits and oligarchs who had appeared and flourished during the mid-1990s, and whose activities had led to the currency default and a widespread drop in living standards. To Russians, their new-found freedom and democracy had amounted to nothing but economic crises, corruption, the birth of the oligarchy and bandit capitalism.

Putin's attraction to the population lies in the stability he has brought to the country, something he vowed to achieve practically with his first presidential utterances. While the tragedies of Russia's not-so-distant past remain fresh in the memory for such a large part of the population, it is not surprising that above all, it is stability – albeit within a system which favours *status quo* over reform – that is prized.

Daniel Kearvell studied History and Russian at the University of Nottingham from 1998 to 2002. He was part of the first British Rugby Team to tour the CIS, and spent his year abroad teaching in Russian schools in St Petersburg and studying Russian in Voronezh. Following graduation, Daniel moved to Moscow to become Commercial Manager for the Russo-British Chamber of Commerce (RBCC). He relocated to St Petersburg to establish and run the RBCC in North-West Russia in 2004. After leaving the Chamber, he joined DHL, where he was responsible for the company's Western Russia operations, before moving on to positions in Brussels, Dubai and Qatar. Daniel is currently based in Romania. He maintains his passion for Russia, and in particular its rugby: the club he founded in 2004, the St Petersburg White Knights, is currently going from strength to strength in the Russian leagues.

The road less travelled

In the 1960s, **Keith Watkinson** *criss-crossed the Eastern bloc to promote British science and technology. The hospitality he received was never less than entertaining*

Between 1945 and 1953, the Soviet Union received a net transfer of resources from the rest of the Eastern Bloc of roughly $14 billion, comparable to the transfer from the United States to Western Europe in the post-war Marshall Plan. Many enterprises were required to sell products at below world prices to the Soviet Union, such as uranium mines in Czechoslovakia and East Germany, coal mines in Poland and oil wells in Romania. Before the Second World War, about 1% – 2% of East Europe's trade was with the Soviet Union. By 1953, this had risen to 37%. In 1947, Stalin denounced the Marshall Plan and forbade participation by all Eastern Bloc countries.

I SPENT most of my working life in Soviet lands. After graduation in 1957, I joined an avionics company specialising in primary and secondary radar. The latter is an identification system to differentiate between friend or foe (IFF) and is highly confidential. Much of my work concerned arranging visits of senior officials from overseas governments to the factory and R&D departments, even though I was not allowed into the R&D building due to lack of security clearance. After a while, it was decided that I should apply for clearance. Some weeks later, my boss called me in and enquired: 'Who are you, Watkinson?' with a smile on his face. He revealed that my security clearance was higher than his. It transpired that National Service in the Royal Navy had already given me high clearance. In the Navy, we were introduced to transmitters and receivers, taught intelligence gathering techniques by listening to, and reporting on, Soviet military radio traffic and service movements. We were also trained in cryptography. The Soviets employed converted deep sea trawlers as listening and reporting posts and tailed our sea exercises. We, in turn, monitored and reported on their traffic. At the end of our training, we had to sign the Official Secrets Act.

In 1964 I joined the country's foremost company in the scientific instrument and laboratory equipment industry in which I spent the rest of my working life. The company was a very active exporter. Initially, I was involved in sales to Western Europe, but subsequently I was made responsible for sales to Communist countries. It was not possible to sell to the Soviet Union directly so the main route was via Soviet-sponsored exhibitions. From our company's side, these were organised by the Scientific Instrument Manufacturers Association of Great Britain (SIMA). The exhibitions were held in the Institute of Physics in central Moscow and were handy for a little sightseeing. The exhibitions were fairly sparsely attended as the local visitors were restricted to scientists and academics nominated by the Academy of Sciences and considered safe to associate with Westerners. None had hard currency and depended on Technoimport, the state trading organisation, to agree to purchase. As the end of the exhibition approached, tension grew among the exhibitors as we waited to see if there would be a sufficient allocation, enough at least to buy the equipment we had taken along with us. As a rule, most of the scientific instruments and laboratory equipment – mainly for chemistry, medical research and the petroleum industry – were purchased.

One evening in 1964 was given over to a reception for our sponsors and other key personages. The guests arrived early and massed in front of the doors to the hall; when they opened, there was a mad dash by the Russians to the buffet table where the throng crowded round, declining to move for anyone, grabbing as much food as they could. This continued until the table was absolutely bare. It was not unusual to spot certain delicacies – bananas, oranges, cheeses, Scotch – stuffed into pockets and taken home. Bananas were favourites, as were oranges. After the food, came the drinking. This was treated with the same enthusiasm. Scotch whisky was knocked back like shots of vodka, but we never saw anyone fall over.

There was a reciprocal reception for us in 1966. In our turn, we homed in on the Beluga caviar and Russian 'champagne' which was some consolation for the appalling food on offer in the hotel. It was customary to stay in the *Ukraina*, a Stalinesque building on the north bank of the Moskva river. The restaurant was extensive, which is more than could be said for the menu. There would be a choice of maybe five or six dishes, inevitably including Chicken Kiev, dumplings and cabbage soup. The service was interminable: two hours for two courses was par. The restaurant had numerous doors through which the waiters would occasionally appear. One evening, impatience got the better of me and I decided to try to search out a waiter. I went through one of the doors only to find myself in a large room which stretched the length of the restaurant and in which stood some twelve or so single, ancient-looking gas cookers; nothing else and no-one to be seen. Beyond that was the kitchen and still no-one. The mind boggled. On another evening, helped by the influence of a Russian acquaintance and an obligatory bribe, we managed to get into reputedly the best restaurant in Moscow, a Georgian one. Whether it was because Stalin was a Georgian or not, it was certainly the best meal I have had in Moscow.

The hotel had some characters who one could imagine were KGB and we were advised to assume the rooms were bugged, the telephones too. All calls were routed through a switchboard, but attempted calls abroad never succeeded. The phone would from time to time ring during the night. If we answered, there was a deafening silence. Each floor had a concierge who monitored comings and goings. That was their sole purpose and they ignored any request for service. The rooms were spacious, but basic. A requisite for guests was to take your own multi-size bath plug, otherwise one had to use a flannel or one's heel, neither of which worked very well. But at least during the depths of winter, when the snow was piled higher than a man's fur hat, the rooms were well heated, often too much so.

The limited spare time outside of work allowed us to do some sightseeing: Red Square, the Kremlin, St. Basil's, the department store GUM, the Moscow Hills and 'Dacha Land', to which Communist Party officials headed *en masse* during the summer. GUM was virtually devoid of goods, but it was possible to buy fur hats, galoshes (essential for when the snow thawed), and nick-nacks such as wooden toys (especially *matrioshki*, nested dolls). Visits to the ballet at the Bolshoi theatre were treats to be savoured.

During the sixties, I travelled regularly to other eastern bloc countries. SIMA organised exhibitions in Hungary and Romania. Hungary was friendlier and the food better, whereas Romania was dismal and the food routinely awful, often comprising cold carp in aspic for dinner. In Poland and Czechoslovakia, we participated in the Poznan and Brno fairs respectively. It was possible to travel more freely in Czechoslovakia, Hungary and Poland than in Russia and the GDR, and I often took my car to these countries, which gave me space for more sensitive equipment. Not once was I stopped by the local police despite anticipating trouble at the border posts. The greatest hazard, especially at night, was the local peasants driving their horse-drawn carts without lights. These carts were constructed from a tree trunk to which planks were attached at an angle of 45 degrees. Laden or unladen, they were a lethal weapon and to be avoided at all costs. The horses always had a hessian sack attached to their rumps to collect the manure to spread on the peasants' vegetable patches.

In Budapest, I often stayed at the Gellert Hotel on the Buda bank of the Danube. Amazingly, for a hotel of its era, it had a rooftop swimming pool. It was also situated next to one of the oldest Turkish baths in the country; a rare accepted legacy of the oppressive, cruel rule of the Turks. I made the mistake of visiting the baths early in the morning before work. They were huge and one had to submit oneself to a series of baths of varying temperatures before plunging into ice cold water. Various forms of massage by burly men were undertaken between baths. I found it almost impossible to stay awake for the rest of that day.

On one occasion, the interpreter allocated to us at the exhibition was a Hungarian woman who spoke with an American accent. During dinner one evening, she gave a graphic account of the Soviet troops' behaviour at the time of the Hungarian uprising. They were mainly 'Mongols', as she put it, and totally ignorant: they drank the perfume they stole and ate toothpaste. Many young women were raped. With a couple of friends, she had fled Hungary in 1956, taking five days to cross the border to Austria – avoiding border police, spies and rogue guides demanding money and then disappearing into the trees. From Austria, she was sent to Sweden and from there she came to the UK and managed to get a job in the American Embassy in London. Some six years later she came under intense pressure from her family to return. As soon as her train crossed the border into Hungary she was taken into custody. On release, she was issued with an ID card which stated she was a 'kept woman'. She was eventually allowed a job and to interpret in controlled circumstances, but bitterly regretted returning to her homeland.

The year 1968 was a testing one for Czechoslovakia, to say the least. I went there several times before the Prague Spring, during it and after the Russian tanks had rolled in. Before, Prague was a pleasant and interesting place. It was reasonably relaxed and almost devoid of tourists, unlike today. During the Prague Spring, the atmosphere was almost euphoric – people were more relaxed and overtly friendly. Nightlife was lively and the bars and restaurants busy. At a meeting at a State Trading Organisation, one of my contacts declared: 'Now we speak with the windows open.' After the arrival of the tanks, it was very oppressive and reminded me of Moscow. The hotels were dreary, the restaurants deserted and officials were loath to meet Westerners. An acquaintance travelled from Brno to see me. His brother, a pastor, had been thrown into prison for objecting to the invasion and he was implicated by association. He left on the night train in tears, asking: 'What are they doing to my country?' I never saw him again.

The reason for my visit was to negotiate a contract for analysis laboratories in an oil refinery to be built overseas. The Czech government had won the contract from the UK before the invasion and payment was to be in hard currency. The Soviet invasion had put off our competitors, who declined to bid. We had submitted a high bid to allow for extra contingencies. The technical negotiations went well, the commercial talks not so well as we refused to reduce the price. As the end of the day approached, the agitation among the Czechs increased. Beer and vodka were produced, which were politely declined. Considerable pressure was put on me to stay until the next day, an impossibility as I had appointments in Frankfurt. The local staff began telephoning home. I understood enough of what was said to gather they were far from happy at being late for their evening meals. I had also gleaned that the Czechs were under enormous pressure from their government to finalise the deal. We were eventually awarded the contract based on our original fee.

In 1968, I was asked to take charge of a new scientific technical information office in Warsaw, Poland, which would operate on behalf of British manufacturers. It could not be a sales office, as it was illegal for a foreign concern to compete with the state organisations. However, it was to all intents and purposes a sales office. I was to move there with my family – my wife and two young daughters, and so one day in early summer saw us on our way in a sturdy Austin 1800 with every available inch of space packed with belongings and essential foods. Anyone who drove across the West German/East German border in those days will remember the bureaucratic tedium of having all one's possessions hauled out of the car and examined in the minutest detail in an ordeal that typically lasted three hours. Once cleared, we had to enter a narrow tunnel with under-car mirrors (in case anyone was clinging to the undercarriage) at the end of which was a massive cannon in case a desperado attempted to drive through without clearance. There was a final check before the barrier was raised. A hundred metres or so further on was the Polish checkpoint where there was a similar procedure, but without tunnel and cannon. In the end, the customs official yielded to the exceptionally warm weather and terminated the procedure.

Our accommodation in Warsaw was an apartment in a block reserved for Westerners. We assumed we were under constant surveillance and it was interesting that Yugoslavs fell into that category too. The building was in the very centre of the city, within walking distance of the major government agencies, the main shops, the Old Town and a pleasant park where a pianist played Chopin on summer Sunday mornings. The working hours were 6am to 2pm or 7am to 3pm due to the fact that offices and factories did not have eating facilities. The main meal was, therefore, at about 4pm. Shops had little to offer: in the case of food shops, they often had nothing at all. Opposite our flat was a butcher's which was often closed for days and on those days when meat was expected the queues started at 6am. Opening times were immaterial and supplies were rapidly exhausted. The Old Town was a treat to visit, though. The original town had been razed during the war and rebuilt according to original plans somehow salvaged from the rubble. The best bargains there were cut glassware – bowls, vases, wine glasses – some of the latter in very fine glass. The lovely buildings housed a variety of artisan workers and their products, bars and restaurants.

My locum boss was the British Ambassador who at the time was Nicholas Henderson - later to be ambassador to Bonn, Paris and Washington. He was tall and slim with grey hair. He was direct, with an excellent grasp of affairs, but approachable and quite affable. On arrival, he welcomed me warmly, told me we could use the social facilities of the Embassy and introduced us to the Principal of the American school where our daughters enrolled. The embassy shop was an absolute boon and we supplemented goods from it by importing from a Danish company which delivered to the shop on a weekly basis. I reported to the ambassador once a week for a mutual briefing and attended his regular 'At Homes' (open house) for visiting British businessmen. On my retirement, an Irishman I met there invited my wife and me to his home in Ireland as a token of his appreciation a full 25 years later.

We decided to return home for Christmas 1969. When we left Warsaw, there was snow on the ground. As we were driving across the plains heading for Poznan, a blizzard developed. The car decided this was a good time to break down after starting to emit smoke. We evacuated it rapidly and once the smoke cleared, looked under the bonnet. It was clearly an electrical fault. The weather had closed in and there was nothing on the road. After some considerable time and as we were becoming very cold, a large *Tatra* hove into view, travelling towards Warsaw. It was chauffeur-driven and clearly a senior East German official's car. The official in the back, very well-dressed, lowered his window and spoke to us in German. I did my best to explain our problem. He looked hard at our two young daughters and said he would get help to us by looking for a telephone wire from the road to a residence. He was as good as his word: later on, a *Warshawa* approached and halted in front of us. Two men emerged. They looked strange with white hair and eyebrows. One look under the bonnet had them sniggering: the leads from the distributor were carbon fibre which they had never seen before. They had only ever seen copper. Nevertheless, they towed us several kilometres before turning into a farmyard and into a barn in which numerous hens strutted about. In the house were two families who warmly welcomed us into their home. The Poles love children and were all over our girls. They could not do enough for them. In the middle of the table was a bowl of oranges. We knew that the Poles could only buy oranges at Christmas, but they insisted that our girls have one each. Eventually tact won out and we were able to avoid making inroads on their annual treat. The two millers offered to drive us back to Warsaw provided we paid in US dollars. This was, of course, illegal but most Westerners had a cache about them somewhere. For $100 we were returned to our flat in Warsaw, where we spent Christmas amid deep snow.

I did not return to Eastern Europe until 1993 when I made a private visit to Poland. Driving past the old immigration post with its frightening fortifications was exhilarating. The new roads, the modern petrol stations, shops which stayed open into the evening and the range and variety of goods on offer, not forgetting the choice of dishes in the restaurants and the dynamism of the people, astounded me.

Keith Watkinson learned Russian in the Royal Navy, after which he read Russian and Slavonic Studies at the University of Nottingham between 1954 and 1957. He pursued a career exporting scientific instruments, travelling extensively to more than 100 countries, and winning, with his company, the Queen's Award for Exports. In the 1960s, he spent considerable time behind the Iron Curtain, including residing in Warsaw for two years. He experienced, at first hand, the height of the Cultural Revolution in China; dodged bullets in the Philippines; and appeared on television with the President of Kenya. He contributed to The Coder Special Archive, *a book about naval servicemen and Russian, published in September 2012.*

High notes, low notes

*Musician **John Culley** conducted a 40-year love-hate affair with Russia, including leading a tour of the country with a youth orchestra and acting as a guide in the Moscow Olympics*

The 1980 Summer Olympics were the first Games to be staged in Eastern Europe. Led by the United States, 65 countries boycotted the Games because of the Soviet Union's war in Afghanistan, This led to the Soviet-led boycott of the 1984 Olympics in Los Angeles. Nevertheless 241 Olympic records were set during the Moscow Olympics as well as 97 world records, and 21% of the competitors were female – a higher percentage than at any previous Olympics.

Curiosity aroused

My affinity with Russia began 40 years ago when my uncle and aunt invited me to join them on a package tour to Moscow. I had begun to learn Russian just a few months before we went. It was a wonderful trip. My uncle was a former RAF tail-gunner in Lancaster bombers. He was an irrepressible entrepreneur and outspoken atheist, but certainly no Communist. However, he had always felt an admiration for the Russian people and their part in the defeat of Nazi Germany, and for the Soviet Union and its technological achievements.

In spite of the efforts of Intourist to paint an idyllic picture of the Soviet state, it was soon clear that there were deficiencies.

Shop windows were devoid of anything interesting. Every time our bus stopped, groups of boys would run to the door shouting 'chewing gum', offering badges in exchange. My aunt had brought spare pairs of tights with her which she offered to various ladies she encountered. Most grateful of all were a couple of lady decorators she spotted through an open door in the corridor of our hotel. Tights were a rare and expensive commodity in 1970s Moscow.

It seemed strange that we were almost discouraged from changing money into roubles. Everything we needed in the hotel could be bought only with foreign currency, and in the 'Beriozka' shops, only open to foreign tourists, to which we were taken after most excursions, roubles were not accepted. Strange too that hardly any Russians seemed to be staying in the hotel. Our guides were dressed smartly, and children wore colourful clothes, but this was in sharp contrast to the dull garments worn by most adults.

One day I left the party and set off on my own to Kalinin Prospekt, where I visited the big 'Melodiia' shop and bought a boxed set of Beethoven's *Fidelio* (sung in Russian), and two copies of the Soviet National Anthem and the 'International'; one for my uncle and one for me. I still have those records in my collection. The drab packaging of the Beethoven set is in sharp contrast to the glossy covers of the LPs sold in the 'Beriozka' stores. Pity I didn't know about the 'Dom knigi' bookstore at the time. Think of the musicians I could have heard perform in 1974: Oistrakh, Rostropovich and Richter, to name but three. Shostakovich, my favourite composer, was still alive.

Intourist booked an evening in the Palace of Congresses for us. It was a performance of *The Barber of Seville,* also in Russian. At the time, I was pleased to understand the line *'Figaro zdes', Figaro tam'*, but the rest was far too hard for me, and I'm sure most of the tourists in the audience found it pretty hard going too. My aunt would dearly have loved to go to the Bolshoi, but even our foreign package tourist status couldn't get us tickets to such a prestigious venue. It didn't occur to us that a suitable bribe in dollars or in western goods might have secured us the best seats in the house.

My enthusiasm for Russia and Russian was heightened by this first visit. I wanted to know what lay behind the façade of this enigmatic country, ostensibly with great political power and enviable social and scientific achievements. I came away with the feeling that, for the average citizen, life in the USSR really wasn't that bad. Only later did I come to understand more about the world of dissidents, persecuted believers of all denominations, and those who simply fell foul of the system for minor transgressions, or just for being in the wrong place at the wrong time.

Memories of student visits in the mid-1970s

In September 1975 I began to read German and Slavonic Studies. After doing Russian A-level from scratch in the VIth form, I knew I wanted to continue my studies in both these languages. One of the main factors in my decision was to get know the language and background of Russian and German composers better.

The trip to Kalinin (now Tver' once again) at the end of my first year of studies was a great way of consolidating my knowledge of Russian. The very name Kalinin took on special significance when it came to light that Yulia Sergeevna, the Soviet assistant at the University of Nottingham for the year 1975-76, was Kalinin's granddaughter.

We stayed in the Hotel Seliger. This was an unforgettable experience in itself. Several rooms shared a single bathroom, for which the key was obtainable only from the ever-present and ever-vigilant *dezhurnaia* (floor warden). The plumbing in the toilets was poor. A notice in beautiful Russian handwriting above the cistern declared *Bumagu v kanalisatsiiu ne brosat'*! (Don't throw paper into the toilet!)

The food was basic, but mostly edible. We had to remind ourselves that people were queuing for hours outside to buy scraggy cuts of meat (if they were lucky) and poor quality vegetables. Our teacher on the summer course was an English department lecturer at the University of Kalinin, and at the end of the course she invited us home for a meal. We were hugely grateful for the chicken meal she had prepared for us, and appreciated the efforts she must have made to buy all the ingredients.

We felt like exotic beings in Russia. When we walked through Kalinin as a group, people stared at us. We were introduced to a group of 'official friends', who must have been particularly good students, as well as good members of the Komsomol. Two of them became my pen-friends for a number of years, and I enjoyed receiving letters in Russian about their studies and the town in which they lived. As soon as they began their professional lives, however, the correspondence stopped.

My year abroad, in the third year of my course, was split between Russia and Germany. I enthusiastically anticipated a stay in Moscow or Leningrad, or even Voronezh (where the Single Honours students went for a whole year), but my hopes were dashed. Thanks to a more or less moribund twinning arrangement, I was sent to Minsk, the Belorussian capital. We travelled by train from Victoria. At the Soviet border, the carriages were still lifted up by steam crane and the bogeys were changed to the broader, Soviet gauge. As we clattered through Belarus, I overheard our conductor ask a local guard what the meat situation was like.

To say that Minsk was not a lively city in the late 1970s is an understatement. Our hostel, on Omsky pereulok, was basic even by Soviet standards. The showers were reminiscent of Zoshchenko's famous *Bania* ('Bathhouse') story, with alternate days for male and female residents, and a day off on Sundays. The washing arrangements for clothes in metal troughs did nothing to encourage personal hygiene. Meanwhile, upstairs in the gents, pipes hung loosely from broken fittings, and piles of bricks on either side of the toilet bowls made lavatory seats unnecessary. Loo paper was, of course, not provided, but local students helpfully left supplies of *Pravda* and *Izvestiia*, in case you forgot to bring your own from the dormitory. The Cuban residents occasionally left their daily paper too, but it was far too shiny to be effective!

At the time, a new Soviet Constitution was being written and President Leonid Brezhnev was in the newspapers daily, and on television for hours on end. TV sets were always on in the common areas of the hostel, but nobody seemed to take any notice of what was being said. Lessons were often dull and uninspiring. A rotund lady called Yadviga Stanislavovna brought some flair to the proceedings when she extolled the virtues of venturing barefoot into the woods while staying at one's dacha. Unfortunately no invitations to join her were extended. Another lecturer called Prokopovich, a professional interpreter, injected some life into lessons too, barking out English translations of typical phrases from the Soviet press in quick-fire succession, and demanding instant translations back into Russian. I had hoped to go to Moscow to visit Mrs Fedorova, our Soviet assistant at the University in the previous year, but my request was turned down by the notorious personnel department.

The 'official friends' in Minsk were less forthcoming than those in Kalinin. They were often distinctly hard going, unwilling to discuss any issues which might be deemed even mildly controversial. I was grateful to one postgraduate student who introduced me to a violin teacher at the Conservatory for Music. She gave me short lessons in between her regular pupils, and I thus met many music students who were less politically-minded than the ones at the foreign language institute.

Some of the British students began to meet the dissident element in Minsk, who congregated at the Yubileinaia Hotel. Another of our number got to know members of a clandestine Baptist church. I was more cautious. A talk from a foreign office official before we left had been very clear about the kind of compromising situations we might encounter in the USSR, and how it was prudent not to get involved in any activity which could be interpreted as anti-Soviet. As I wanted to return to Russia in the future, I kept my contacts to just one or two individuals, and was careful not to introduce one friend to another unless it was clear that they had already met and knew about me. There was still a possibility that people would inform on each other, and citizens who had an interest in Westerners were regarded with suspicion by the Soviet authorities. In the case of the religious groups, the members were simply keen to meet other Christians, but during our stay we heard how some of them had lost their jobs in Minsk and been sent to more remote areas to work.

When I contracted flu-like symptoms and a bad earache, I experienced the Soviet health system at first hand. The Soviet Union boasted more doctors per head of population than any other country in the world. However, when I went to the polyclinic I soon learned that none of these doctors was actually a GP as we know them. I was sent from an ear specialist to a throat specialist, and so on, necessitating long waits each time, and eventually left with a large collection of tablets of various shapes and sizes. In the end, a period of rest and a herbal concoction provided by some Estonian teachers living in our part of the hostel seemed preferable to the plethora of tablets from the polyclinic.

The canteen in the hostel was dreadful. The food was unappetising; knives were rarely available. Smartly-dressed ladies with bee-hive hairstyles skewered pieces of rubbery meat (on offer only occasionally) or the ubiquitous *tefteli* (meatballs) on aluminium forks, and gnawed at them in an ungainly way. Only the *borshch* (beetroot soup) was vaguely palatable, depending on the freshness of the batch and the quality of the piece of gristle which was ceremonially dropped into each portion as we passed along the queue.

Since our monthly grant was at least three times that of our Belorussian counterparts, and we could get currency by changing money or travellers' cheques at the Yubileinaia we were able to eat out in restaurants on a regular basis. The menus were often large, boasting an impressive array of dishes. However, only those dishes with prices printed next to them were likely to be available, and even then it was common for the waiters to inform us that even those were no longer to be had, and we would have to take the *bifshteks* – another version of the ubiquitous meatball.

At least beer and vodka were always available. In fact a bottle of vodka and bottles of beer were usually put on the table before we ordered. In 1985, Gorbachev was to introduce his *sukhoi zakon* (dry law) and this practice was stopped. A number of rather sickly and insipid fizzy drinks were introduced across the empire in an effort to discourage alcohol consumption, but few of them were successful.

The shops were poorly stocked. People queued in the local butcher's, where occasionally a large piece of meat was being chopped up. Buyers seemed to get three refusals on the lump being cut off as they approached the counter. If they didn't like the look of any of it, they went to the back and joined the queue again. We were surprised to see a consignment of Dutch frozen chickens on sale one day. Just as the Dutch football team at the time could beat the Soviet Union (a nation of about sixteen million against one of about 240 million), so that same small country was catering for the food market in a land which really should have been able to provide its own meat.

Essex descends on the Soviet Union (New Year 1978-79)

I had often wondered what it would be like to accompany friends who knew no Russian and very little about the USSR to some of the places I had visited as part of my studies. Now I had my chance. I joined the Essex Youth Orchestra to play and interpret on their tour of Minsk, Moscow and St Petersburg. My musical friends would be able to savour that characteristic smell of petrol or cheap two-stroke fuel which greeted you as soon as you got out of the airport terminal, or enjoy the less pleasant odour of unwashed Russians in the Metro, as decent soap and other cosmetics were so hard to come by.

The tour also coincided with one of the coldest winters since the Second World War. In Leningrad the heating was only working properly on one side of the hotel. On the overnight train from Moscow to Minsk we occupied three carriages: one had good heating, one had some, but the third was like a fridge.

During our stay in Moscow it was so cold that one day tourists in the smart hotels for foreigners were warned not to go outside. As we were staying in a less prestigious establishment, the 'Orlionok' on Lenin Hills, we had been given no such warning. We toured the Kremlin at -29 C.

As a youth orchestra, we were treated to a number of the usual dull tours, including my second visit to the Minsk fridge factory, and the Belorussian National Museum. There was little provision for rehearsal time in the schedule. Our guides always seemed astonished when we tried to excuse ourselves from the excursions, explaining that we needed to practise before performances. Since no orchestras like the County Youth Orchestra existed in the USSR, we were not given the status of touring musicians. As a youth group, we had to endure the tours as a compulsory element in the programme.

There were a few opportunities to meet Russian music students, which we all enjoyed very much. They were often amazed that amateur musicians were able to tackle major works of the symphonic repertoire. Some of these were unscheduled, as the itinerary seldom ran to plan. Publicity was poor, and in one venue we were billed as a folk-group. So it was not surprising that some members of the audience walked out during our first piece, which was Berlioz's 'Roman Carnival Overture'.

At an evening reception with Komsomol members in Leningrad, I got myself into a rather awkward corner, when one of our hosts asked me to give examples of things I didn't like about the USSR. Not wishing to cause offence, I suggested that the shop-assistants were unfriendly. 'Unfriendly?' he replied sarcastically. 'If you'd been here sixty years ago, they'd have shot you.'

One evening I took two friends into the city centre by trolleybus and Metro. The trolley-bus driver was astonished to have 'rich Westerners' on his bus, even remarking that we should have gone by taxi. After visiting the bar in the Intourist Hotel, we decided to take a taxi back to the Lenin Hills after all. In Soviet days, taxi drivers seemed to have fixed routes. That night, none of the drivers actually wanted to go in our direction – certainly not for roubles anyway. We eventually found a driver who would drive us for dollars. It was more expensive but we got back a lot quicker than if we had attempted the journey by public transport.

Live at the Moscow Olympics (Summer 1980)

I heard that the tour company charged with getting British tourists to the summer Olympics in 1980 were looking for Russian speakers to accompany the many parties due to be going. I was given an interview at the offices of the travel company David Dryer Sports in London and was delighted to be selected as one of the guides. About 30 coach-loads were due to go, but after the Soviet invasion of Afghanistan the number of coaches fell to three. I was charged with accompanying one coach on my own.

I met my party at Victoria Coach Station, and we travelled to Calais by ferry where the Soviet Intourist bus was due to meet us. The journey to Moscow was to take several days with one overnight stay in Warsaw and three in Minsk, although Minsk was also an Olympic venue. The party comprised a mixed bag of people. For many, this was not their first Olympics. There was a teacher with his wife and two children, three retired bus drivers from Scotland, a factory worker from Kent, a mother and her twenty-something daughter, and a couple of groups of young men from England and Wales. Two of the more unusual characters on a British bus were a white South African man who worked in Cologne and a black African from Zambia. They all got on very well together. One elderly gentleman sometimes irritated the party by wandering off on his own at almost every stop. He never went far away, but his sense of time-keeping was poor.

In Calais we waited for our coach in vain, and I phoned the David Dryer office from a French pay-phone (no mobiles in those days of course). I was advised to hang on, and to assure the tourists that all would be fine. When the bus eventually arrived, the drivers explained that they had been issued with an old map and had gone to the wrong port, the former ferry terminal.

Noticing that there was a roll of carpet in the back of the bus and evidence of other shopping, I suspected that they had made the most of their time in the West and had been out on a buying spree. The bus was of Western design, and had all the necessary comforts for a long journey, but for some reason our two drivers were reluctant to run the hot water for drinks all the time; they also wanted notice if we wished to visit the loo. They must have been trying to economise on water and energy consumption.

Crossing the borders of Western Europe was not easy for a Russian bus. Our drivers had to show all their documents, and various toll charges had to be paid. As we penetrated further east their passage became easier and we, the British tourists, were subjected to ever more scrupulous checks.

On the third day we arrived at Brest-Litovsk, the Soviet border. Here we were subjected to the most stringent customs check yet. A young couple in our party had exchanged suitcases and ran into problems as a result. The female customs officer opened the heavy case that the man was carrying and proceeded to wave items of ladies' underwear in front of him and to display them to her colleagues. The man tried to explain that they belonged to his girlfriend, but the official didn't appear to understand. I was called over to interpret, and eventually the matter was cleared up, but the officials were not happy about the swap of luggage.

Once through customs we were met by our Soviet guide who accompanied us for the rest of the trip. Owing to the international boycott, there were so few Olympic events in Minsk that we were treated to a tour of the fridge factory – my third in four years.

Moscow was tidied up for the games and nearly all children were obliged to spend the Olympic period at pioneer camps. The British group was shielded from the worst exigencies of Soviet Russia. Makeshift painted fencing had been put up around the old wooden housing in parts of Minsk and Moscow. Yet it was probably the monotonous tower blocks which the tourists would have found least attractive.

There was an exciting atmosphere at the games, with most national groups allocated seats together. As the boycotting nations were only able to receive medals to the playing of the international Olympic anthem, the small pockets of their supporters would often strike up the national anthem from their part of the stadium. There was a feeling of camaraderie among those who had defied the political boycott in order to support the athletes and the spirit of international sporting endeavour.

The three retired Scottish bus drivers came in a panic to find me one evening. They had tried to buy drinks in the bar with Scottish bank notes. 'He wudnae take ma money, John,' one of them exclaimed. The barman had searched through his official book illustrating foreign bank notes, but clearly the illustrations of Bank of Scotland notes had not made it into the weighty tome he had at his disposal. Someone else from the group changed the money for them and they were happy until they discovered the drinks cost at least three times more than the UK price. Another of our party was a rather scruffy man from Kent. He was of large build and wore a shabby brown sports jacket even on the hottest days. The various door-keepers would supervise our entry into hotels and restaurants, usually letting us all through without question, but this one particular man was nearly always stopped and challenged for ID. He looked 'ordinary enough' to be a Russian, and I regularly had to explain that he was indeed a member of our group.

On the return journey, the food in a West German motorway service station had never tasted so good. We arrived in the nick of time for our ferry, leaving a large hard currency tip for the drivers, who had done a good job on the whole. The rather officious Soviet guide left us in Minsk, but she was less impressed with the bottle of Soviet perfume which I had bought with the rouble collection we made for her before leaving Soviet territory. It may have been the most expensive thing in the hotel rouble shop, but it wasn't what she expected from Western tourists. Still, she might have thought twice about the fridge factory the next time.

Despite all that, I had only managed to get to the Games once, but it was the memorable Coe-Ovett 800m final. I sat a few rows behind Henry Cooper and thoroughly enjoyed a captivating spectacle.

Plus ça change...Gorbachev's USSR (Summer 1987)

By 1987, Gorbachev was in power and things were beginning to change in the USSR. I applied for a place on the course for foreign teachers of Russian in Leningrad and really enjoyed the opportunity to be back in Russia and to visit some sights and places I had never seen before.

There was the usual Soviet approach to foreigners: our rooms were away from those of any Russians who may still have been there over the summer, and all the teaching was done in national groups. As there were Hungarian, Yugoslav and even French groups, it would have been interesting and productive to take some of the courses together, but that was seldom done.

Our stay also coincided with the visit of a group of American Russian teachers. In the spirit of *perestroika* they had been invited to participate on the course as some of the first American teachers of Russian to visit the Soviet Union in an official capacity. They were duly accorded a reception with the President himself in the Kremlin and we heard the American group leader speaking on Russian radio. '*My prosto vo vostorge*,' (We are delighted), he said with a heavy American accent.

At the Institute of Foreign Languages we were even allowed to take part in an open discussion of the Soviet Union: all in the spirit of *glasnost'* and *perestroika*. When invited to criticise what we had seen so far, I said I found the state of public toilets appalling. (The ones in the Novgorod coach park had been particularly awful). Instead of a stock Soviet response, the lecturer actually sympathised, and admitted that much was still to be achieved. More overtly political questions were still not given very open responses and it was still pointless to pursue issues of human rights or free and open elections. But the overall atmosphere of the discussion was far more forthcoming and honest than anything I had experienced in the Soviet Union before.

On a tour of the Menshikov Palace we were shown a beautiful salon with a harpsichord and a grand piano. The guide told us that recitals were often given there. I asked where we could get tickets, only to be told the recitals were open only to members of the Academy of Music. This was a typical example of *klass* at work in the Soviet Union. During that same stay, we visited the best restaurant I had ever experienced in Russia. The restaurant was located in the House of Architects, a large building without any obvious name-board outside to advertise it. The décor was fairly plain, but tasteful, and the waiters were efficient and attentive. We would never have been able to go there had we not met someone with connections in the architectural field. The food was tastier than in ordinary Russian restaurants, although the selection of dishes was similar. I also went to a showing of a Tarkovsky film (*The Sacrifice*, which had been shot in Sweden), again because I had been fortunate enough to meet an artist with connections in the film and theatre world.

Other restaurants and clubs more often than not still displayed the ever-present *Mest net* (No room) sign, and it seemed that only bribery or connections would grant access. We sometimes made do with *pelmeni* (a kind of Russian ravioli) from a very shabby looking café near the Griboedov Canal; the most expensive variety was served with sour cream, the cheapest with vinegar. The Beer Bar on the other side of the Griboedov Canal, opposite the preposterously named Museum of Religion and Atheism (at St Isaac's Cathedral) was also worth a visit. Each round of drinks was accompanied by a plate of *zakuski* (snacks). The pretzels had to be smashed on the table to break them. The smoked fish were so obdurate that they needed a couple of slaps on the table followed by several minutes of manipulation before you were able to break off small morsels to eat with your beer. The beer itself was quite palatable. As in Kalinin eleven years before, there were still no bars where all kinds of drinks were available. For that you had to have dollars and preferably a hotel *propusk* (pass).

Post-communist Russia: signs of change (1993-95)

My first trip to post-Communist Russia was with a group from the Westcliff High School for Boys in the winter of 1993 and, while the country looked much the same, I found that the style of guiding had changed considerably. We gave the boys numbers and they counted themselves present in Russian, much to the delight of the guide. She also obliged us by giving the Russian names for the sites. I think we were lucky to find such a good guide. In Soviet times they either spoke English or Russian, but they would refuse to mix the two in order to help pupils who were learning the language. Before 1991 it was no doubt to do with official scripts; in post-Communist Russia they can still be rather obstinate, probably due to the poor rate of pay. Different prices for museum visits and guided tours for locals and foreigners still persist and foreigners are charged often three to ten times more at theatres, museums or sights than Russian citizens.

The large banners and bill-boards of Soviet times with party slogans had all but disappeared. Shop signs were beginning to look more attractive and advertising was starting to appear everywhere.

During the trip we arranged to meet a teacher of English and some of her pupils in our hotel foyer. Although she had been teaching English for nearly ten years, she said that she had never met 'real English people' before. On the strength of this meeting we visited her school, and a school exchange was established.

My trip in Spring 1994 was my second orchestral tour in Russia. Andrew Constantine, the founder and erstwhile conductor of the Bardi Orchestra, had studied with the legendary Ilya Musin[9] in St Petersburg, so it was a pleasure for him to take his own orchestra back to the city where he had studied. The Bardi Orchestra was made up of amateur and semi-professional players including a number of music teachers, many of whom had been members of the Leicestershire Schools Symphony Orchestra in the past. I used to drive up to Leicester from Stamford to play viola and I made a welcome return to the orchestra for this tour. We played in the Hermitage Theatre and in the Hall of the Philharmonic, and there were many memorable musical

---

[9] Russian conductor and theorist of conducting (1904-99)

moments.

Russia was coming to terms with capitalism. Various baggage handlers approached us at the airport, all asking for a fee to unload the double basses. Unable to decide which ones were genuine, we were reluctant to pay or bribe any of them. We must have prevaricated too long, for at this point a double bass in its heavy wooden travel 'coffin' came flying through the rubber luggage curtain. It must have taken an enormous effort to throw such a heavy item. One of our bass-players screamed in horror. The bass was slightly damaged – no joke when a reasonable bass can cost at least £3,000. But fortunately the rest were delivered securely. I don't think any money changed hands, but the baggage handlers had made their point. Russia was still a country in which service had to be paid or haggled for. No job was done at face value.

The newly-floated rouble was losing value on the international exchange market. One evening in the hotel bar a group of Italians were jubilant, because for once a lira exchange rate appeared as 1 – 1. There were about 3,000 new roubles to the pound. In the hotel, this would buy a beer or a shot of vodka, but it may have been worth slightly more in the Russian shops. Money changers were still operating in the city and our musical director was tricked into taking too few notes for his sterling by a dodgy operator on the street. Some of the notes in a wad had been folded in two, so when half the pile was flicked through it seemed like the right sum. Only on closer inspection did he find himself to be a few thousand roubles short.

It was still quite normal in those days to flag down a car and offer to pay for a lift to your destination. The system seemed to work well and was certainly cheaper than using the services of the persistently mercenary taxi-drivers. It would take a few more years for them to learn about customer service.

Spring 1995 saw my first stay in a Russian flat. For the current generation it seems unthinkable that in Soviet times it was virtually impossible to stay in a Russian home. I visited one or two flats, but never actually slept in one overnight. Now I was able to experience life in a Russian block of flats for myself, and enjoy homemade Russian cuisine. I learned that one left dishes served up for the evening meal at one's peril; they would be sure to be served again for breakfast. One morning a bowl of cold beetroot salad was on the breakfast plate. The lady of the house had had to go out early, and that was all she left for me and her son.

Moscow and back in four disastrous days (July 2008)

Trips to Russia can still be an ordeal, even in recent times, as I was to discover in the summer of 2008, on my twenty-eighth visit. I had applied for a job at an English language school in Moscow. The company was Russian, with a head office quite near Red Square, although the lessons took place in various venues around the city and mostly in 'twilight hours'. I was interviewed over the phone by another teacher of English as a foreign language. The job offer came shortly afterwards.

However, as the date to commence work approached, I had begun to get a little concerned. The school had sent me virtually no information about my timetable or the levels I might be teaching, and friends in Russia had already warned me that the prospective salary seemed very low. They had also not heard of the company. It was not an auspicious start to a planned nine-month's stay.

I boarded the plane with a sense of adventure, and the hope of an exciting and rewarding time in Moscow. The flight was reasonably uneventful: just a double-booked seat, and extra flying time because of a storm. A driver met me to take me to the flat.

It turned out to be in an area of Moscow I didn't know. I had asked for accommodation in the north of the city. This flat was in the east, and almost at the end of a Metro line. The accommodation manager rang to check if everything was alright, and told me I would be on my own that evening, although another teacher would be arriving the following week to share the flat.

She also said that someone would come to collect me at 8.30 the following morning.

The driver stopped at a shop where I was able to buy provisions for the next day. The school had provided a 'starter pack' with money and Metro and phone cards, as promised. But the driver struggled to find the address. Eventually we discovered it some way from the main road, where the street lighting was poor.

I climbed to the fourth floor and the driver set about trying to unlock the door. After much effort it opened, and I got my first look at the flat. The two rooms were totally different in size. I decided to take the larger one because it had a television. It didn't have a proper bed – just an L-shaped sofa. The driver handed me a plastic bag containing new sheets and pillow cases, and left. I locked the door from the inside, checking that both the locks on the outside door were in place. The inner door had no lock. Both were broken.

Closer inspection of the flat was a bitter disappointment. I was not prepared for the amount of junk left by previous occupants. There were piles of dirty bed linen, blankets, pillows and other things left in the cupboards; the drawers in the dressing table were broken, and there was a general lack of cleanliness, especially in the kitchen. The balcony was full of rubbish.

I sent a text to a good friend in Germany and she rang me back just as I was opening the fridge, which had a broken shelf and appeared, judging by the smell, to have been turned off for some time. I discovered that it was unplugged. The previous occupant had left a microwave oven and that was plugged in but, as there was only one electric socket in the kitchen, it appeared that you could either use the oven or the fridge, but not both at the same time. I rummaged around behind the fridge and inserted the plug on the end of a dirty and dusty wire. It began to work noisily. Luckily my room was on the other side of the flat.

After talking to my German friend and giving her a running commentary on the fridge and the state of the kitchen, I attempted to ring my old friend, Kirill, in Khimki. As I almost expected by this time, I couldn't get through. Things just weren't going my way.

I continued to explore. The bathroom was dingy and in need of decoration. The shelf above the basin was loose and the toilet seat was only attached on one side. The mat should have been thrown away years before. The shower curtain had also seen better days.

I unpacked my pyjamas and considered hanging up some things in the wardrobe. But the smell of the bedding that had been left inside made me decide to leave them in my case for the time being. I chose a pillow which wasn't too smelly, put one of the new cases on it, and settled down for the night. I was very tired. A hideous electric clock, with a photo of two kittens on it, ticked away noisily in the background. When I eventually fell asleep, it was only to wake up again up after no more than an hour. In the bathroom, the toilet was still flushing. I fiddled with the lever and eventually the water stopped. Now I could finally get some sleep, I thought.

But I did not sleep well. The clock with the kittens annoyed me all night. I was beginning to consider a rapid exit, or at least changing the flat. When I got up at about 7am, I saw the place in its full glory in the morning light - dirty and ragged curtains, wallpaper beginning to peel, and a general air of neglect. Only the television worked. 8.30am came. 9am passed. Still no one had arrived. I phoned the office, but the person I needed to speak to was not going to be there till 10am, presumably for my own appointment.

The doorbell rang. By this time I had started to pack. I tried to unlock the door, but it refused to budge. I grazed my thumb in the process and a large blister came up. The young lady who had been sent to take me to the central office suggested that I throw the keys out of the window so that she could try to open the door from the outside. I stepped on to the rickety balcony and threw them down to her. She couldn't open the door either, so she phoned for a mechanic. I paced around the flat in a state of utter frustration. I decided to pack everything and go to the office with my belongings. The young lady had one more go at opening the door just as the mechanic was entering the building and this time she succeeded. It would be impractical to take my things with me to the office, she said, so we set off for the Metro, leaving the mechanic to repair the lock.

The walk to the Metro took 40 minutes. I enjoyed chatting to the very attractive young lady, but told her that I should probably not be staying. Although she tried to persuade me to give things a go, saying that the flat was not so bad, she admitted she wanted to leave Russia herself and work abroad. She was disturbed by the social inequalities in the country and the fact that only in Moscow were people reasonably affluent. She warned me about pick-pockets on the Metro and said it was essential to lock the flat door when inside, because of the high level of crime in the city.

It was a long journey to the office; my guide missed our stop and we arrived over two hours late. The recruitment manager said they couldn't offer me a new flat, suggesting that the one I had been given was one of the better ones. She intimated that if I was unhappy it would be best to go now, as it would be harder to leave later – a multiple entry visa would take three weeks and would cost more. She said the school had plenty of teachers, so my services were not that important to them. This was clearly not the time to claim that I should get more money in view of my experience and qualifications!

The leaving process was easy. I just had to pay back the money from the advance the previous day and ring from the flat so that someone could come for the key. However, my troubles were not over. When I got back to the flat, the lock was jammed again. I phoned the office and waited for the mechanic to reappear. Outside it began to pour with rain. I stood at a window on the landing and in desperation phoned my friends at Khimki. They were very understanding and said I could come to their place and then go on to the airport with them. The taxi fare to Khimki cost €150. The Azerbaijani taxi driver stopped twice – once to change money and once to pick up his mobile from the repairer's. At one of the stops he was good enough to stop the meter.

With the help of my Russian friends, I was able to find a place to buy a very cheap ticket to Germany – where fortunately I was still renting a flat – on Siberian Airlines. At €230 it was not much dearer than the taxi fare across Moscow. After buying the ticket, I decided to go to my favourite music shop. It was shut 'for technical reasons'. Moscow was not smiling on me.

There was a 'welcome back barbecue party' waiting for me at my friends' home in Wackernheim. It had been my shortest visit to Russia and one I shall not soon forget. But my love of travel to the country remains undiminished.

John Culley lives in his native Essex, settling back in Rayleigh in 2010. He works as a peripatetic string teacher for Thurrock and Southend Music Services and teaches languages privately. He performs regularly as an orchestral musician and singer in numerous local amateur and semi-professional ensembles. He also returns to Germany regularly where he acts as a linguistic adviser for a friend's aviation consultancy business.